Your Boss

Is Not

Your Mother

ALSO BY BRIAN DES ROCHES:

Reclaiming Yourself: The Codependent's Recovery Plan

Your Boss *Is Not* Your Mother

Creating Autonomy, Respect, and
Success at Work

Brian DesRoches, Ph.D.

William Morrow and Company, Inc.
New York

It s the policy of William Morrow and Company, Inc., and its imprints and affiliates, recognizing the importance of preserving what has been written, to print the books we publish on acid-free paper, and we exert our best efforts to that end.

DesRoches, Brian, 1946–
Your boss is not your mother : creating autonomy, respect, and success at work
by Brian DesRoches.
p. cm.
·ISBN 0-688-11763-5
1. Managing your boss. 2. Interpersonal relations. 3. Conflict
management. I. Title.
HF5548.83 .D47 1995
650.1—dc20 94-21233
CIP

Printed in the United States of America

First Edition

1 2 3 4 5 6 7 8 9 10

BOOK DESIGN BY CLAIRE VACCARO

This book is dedicated to my wise and wonderful wife, Patti, and my two precious children, David and Christine. Thank you for lighting up the days of my life.

Acknowledgments

Many people have accompanied me in the process of writing this book. Some have contributed their stories; others, their expertise. All have provided support and encouragement in a variety of ways.

First of all, I want to thank all the clients and workshop participants who shared their struggles and hopes with me. Your openness and desire to change your experiences at work inspired and empowered me. I hope this book further supports you in empowering yourself.

I am deeply appreciative to the staff of the Montlake Institute, especially Fred Wardenburg and the late Nancy Czech, for giving me new eyes with which to see myself and the world of families and organizations.

I want to gratefully acknowledge the feedback and support of my colleagues Thomy Barton and Charlie Pinkava. They offered different perspectives that helped me see more clearly what I wanted this book to say.

I also want to thank many friends and colleagues for affirming the importance of this book from the very beginning—Susan Grisham, Trisha Pearce, Shelton Huettig, Stuart Dautoff, Hellen Hemphill,

Ph.D., Frank Hoffman, M.D., Yasha, Glenn Leichman, Ph.D., Alexandra Kovats, CSJP, and Richard Anderson, Ph.D. And although it is late in coming, many thanks to Rita Bresnahan, Ph.D., for her inspiration and openness.

The encouragement of my agent Candice Fuhrman and the editorial skills and vision of Jody Rein were once again essential elements on this journey. I also want to acknowledge Carol Costello and Kris Freeman.

I want to thank Will Schutz, Ph.D., for his permission to adapt the material from Element-B survey as part of this book. His books provide a uniquely practical and innovative approach to interpreting the way we interact in the workplace.

The writings and research of Edwin Friedman, Ph.D., and the late Murray Bowen, M.D., have been instrumental in my thinking about families, family process, and the workplace. Despite their critical roles in conceptualizing and testing the theories and ideas in this book, I take complete responsibility for its contents.

There are a few more people that I would like to thank for their indirect involvement in this book's creation. They include Bill Novosedlik, Robert G. Dunn, Pat Otis, and the late Donald Danielson. Thank you for being there when I needed you.

Author's Note

The examples involving the personal lives of people have been taken from real-life experiences and situations. Stories from several individuals have been merged in the interests of providing more information and ensuring confidentiality. In addition, names and occupations have been changed to protect the confidentiality of the individuals involved.

Contents

Contents

Part Three
MAKING CHANGES:
SIX ACTION STEPS

Introduction

Most of us spend at least half of our adult lives at work. To get our jobs done, we must interact with other people. It's easy to take these work relationships for granted. I think that's a big mistake. Problems within work relationships create obvious, damaging stresses for us. Not only do they cause us to dislike our work, they are counterproductive to both our individual health and the health of the organization.

I believe we deserve better than that, and I have found a simple, effective way to make work relationships happier, more supportive, and more productive.

The buzzwords in American business today may be teamwork and communication; each is crucial to empowering a more efficient and creative work force to compete in the global economy—*but we still haven't figured out how to get along with one another at the office.* Corporations spend billions each year on consultants and training programs to enhance communication and management skills, but how we relate to one another doesn't seem to improve much. What we're doing simply isn't working.

I believe this is because we're tackling the wrong problems and look-ing in all the wrong places for solutions. This book offers a new ap-proach that grew out of my experience in business, my study of family systems therapy, and my work as a psychotherapist and organizational systems consultant.

◙ STAFF MEETINGS LIKE THANKSGIVING DINNERS

Unlike most psychotherapists, I spent many years working in busi-ness settings: hospital administration, health-care marketing and plan-ning, management consulting, and training and development. I've spent hundreds of hours in staff meetings that had all the emotional el-ements of a stressful Thanksgiving dinner with the family, except that no turkeys were thrown across the room. I know what it's like to be stuck in "the system" and frustrated by it.

In the mid-1980s, I began to focus my psychotherapy practice on people's difficulties in work situations. I soon noticed a striking sim-ilarity between the problems my clients had with people at work and those they had experienced in their families as children. I decided to take a closer look and embarked upon a two-year study of this phe-nomenon, conducting focus groups and corporate seminars, testing new ideas, and working with clients to implement the approaches I was developing. I researched this subject in the diverse fields of psy-chology, organizational development, management, and family sys-tems. I had numerous consultations with career consultants, staff-development and training specialists, and other therapists. I con-cluded that not only were my observations about people's interactions in organizations accurate, very little had been written about this crit-ical subject. Clearly there was a connection between how people dealt with stressful interactions at work and how stressful situations had been handled in their families. Moreover, I learned that most compa-nies unknowingly encourage the problems that make work relation-ships so stressful.

Since 1989, I have directed about seventy-five seminars on this new approach, for clients in aerospace, software, medical and professional services, government, and manufacturing. My clients included individuals, small entrepreneurial firms, and large corporations.

This book brings together everything I've learned and lays out my approach so that individuals can understand and use it on their own. This material is not intended to replace therapy or to oversimplify extremely difficult work situations or personal backgrounds. I simply propose a new way of looking at work relationships that empowers people to grow as unique, autonomous individuals, even while working within the system.

▣ THE SYSTEMS APPROACH

There are two basic ways to resolve problems among people. The first focuses on finding out who is to blame and doing whatever we can to minimize that person's impact on us: we ignore, fire, or avoid the problem person, or we attempt to change his or her behavior. The trouble is that although the person may go away, the problems don't. They may seem to disappear temporarily, but like a beach ball held underwater, they resurface over and over—often in even more powerful forms.

The second approach is to see people and the problems they experience as linked together in a complex web or system of interactions and relationships. All the elements in the system—individual personalities, past history, what is said and done, feelings, relationships—are interdependent and have reciprocal effects on one another. The system has a life of its own, and no one individual is to blame for any particular problem. Everything in the system affects us, just as we affect everything in it.

Using this systems approach, you resolve difficulties by understanding the system itself rather than by concentrating on how individuals behave. Defining and dealing with the problem itself becomes more important than deciding who is to blame. You begin to notice patterns of behavior within the system that give rise to problems, and to look at how you can change those patterns, rather than focusing on how you can change or punish individuals who are only *parts* of those patterns. This gives you the power to find effective solutions.

◙ FAMILIES AND ORGANIZATIONS

Until now, the systems approach has been applied primarily to re-solving difficult relationships in families. Family systems therapy—the idea that families are systems in which all the people and elements are interdependent and affect one another—has enjoyed wide acceptance over the past fifteen years. Traditional therapies had focused on the "problematic" individual; family systems therapy also considers the context in which that individual functions—the family's emotional system and his or her relationships with other family members. Family systems therapy gives people an understanding of how problems are generated and enormously effective tools with which to solve them.

This book is the first to apply the dynamic, proven principles of family systems therapy to the problems that individuals experience in their work environments. I propose that *organizations function just like families, and that applying the systems approach to the problems and challenges of work relationships can be just as effective as it is in families.*

We acknowledge the existence of emotional systems in families but often ignore emotional realities in the workplace. We act as if people don't have feelings or emotional interactions once they walk through the doors at work, and as if these feelings and interactions don't affect the way they do their jobs.

I suggest not only that a very powerful emotional system operates in each workplace but also that each of us takes to work patterns of relating that we learned in our families and replicates them in stressful relationships there.

◙ TAKING CHARGE

The essence of my approach is this: Learn how your organization, like your family, functions as an emotional system. Identify the patterns of interaction that can be used in both systems to deal with stressful, difficult, or conflict-filled situations. Discover and be alert to the unique patterns and specific habitual reactions you experienced in your family system, and assess whether or not you are repeating them in your office's emotional system. Understand that you do have the ability to change how your organization functions by changing how you function within it. Make a plan and change your behavior. When you change yourself, you change the system. You've broken free.

This book presents that approach in three parts:

- Part 1 is about how family patterns originate and function, why they surface at work under stress, and how they fuel the emotional environment in your organization, work team, or office.

- Part 2 is about identifying your own family patterns and understanding what triggers them. You'll learn how to predict when you're heading for trouble, figure out what is causing the problem, and get yourself out of it.

- Part 3 is my six-step approach to making specific changes in your situation. It offers exercises that map the emotional environments in your office and your family, assess the risks involved in making changes, help you decide exactly what changes to make, and plan strategies that give you the best chance for success.

It boils down to this: *Understand* what's causing your problem at work, *pinpoint* your contribution to the problem, and *change* what you can. It's clear, but not always easy. This book clarifies the process, leads you through each step of the transformation, and gives you the tools to take charge of any situation or relationship.

Success and self-esteem are about knowing that you have choices. Whenever you experience choices in how you relate with others, your ability to govern and direct your life is greatly enhanced. An inner sense of autonomy and freedom grows. You are able to view yourself with greater understanding and take proactive steps to make choices abut your life. The self-awareness, autonomy, and self-respect you experience will show up in your relationships as you experience others with greater objectivity. You will create a successful work life that combines an empowering sense of autonomy with a positive feeling of respect for others.

I hope, if you get nothing else from this book, you learn that you do have choices in how you relate with people at work. With that knowledge, you can make and implement choices that create healthy, productive, and supportive relationships.

◨ THE PEOPLE IN THIS BOOK

The people described in this book are not sick or even unusual; they are just trying to deal with stressful relationships at work. Their situations represent a cross section of the kinds of problems that people face in organizations today. In describing their situations and solutions, I've often cut to the chase and presented their answers without going over all the ground they and I covered together, merely to save time and illustrate a point. Nobody's situation is simple, and nobody's solutions are pat. These courageous people did a great deal of work to find their answers, and they deserve the rewards they are enjoying today—richer, more respectful and enjoyable relationships with bosses, coworkers, and staff. My hope is that you find that same rich reward.

Three of the key elements in the art of working together are how to deal with change, how to deal with conflicts and how to reach our potential.

—Max De Pree
Leadership Is an Art

Compassion is the keen awareness of the interdependence of all things.

—Thomas Merton

Part One

ONE

BIG HAPPY FAMILY?

HOW

FAMILY PATTERNS

WORK

In Part 1, we will explore how the emotional systems in organizations often resemble those in families—and how, when relationships at work become stressful, people are likely to adopt the same defensive strategies they learned as children to deal with stress in the family system.

We will look at the dynamics of these emotional systems: how they get started, how they operate, and what keeps them in place.

1

The Family Across Your Desk

Tom left his boss Jack's office feeling angry and embarrassed. This was the third time Jack had avoided the issue of a raise when Tom brought it up. Back at his desk, Tom seethed as he fantasized about walking out and never coming back.

Instead he indulged in a half hour of boss-bashing with his colleague Shirley and left for an early lunch.

In my office the next day, he felt guilty and confused. "I can't believe it. I rehearsed what I was going to say to him for three weeks. I was ready for anything. But when he grinned and asked me how I liked the new phone system, I lost it. I was like a kid throwing a tantrum, shouting that he was out of touch with what was going on. No wonder he told me to leave and come back when I had cooled down. It's like I'm hard-wired to do crazy things around that guy."

Tom was an extremely capable middle manager, well liked and respected by his peers and staff. He worked hard, liked his job, and seemed to have everything going for him—except that whenever he tangled with Jack, he found himself rebelling, sulking, and generally feeling and acting like a six-year-old. He should have been having a great time and enjoying tremendous success, but instead he felt stuck and demoralized. His relationship with Jack was undermining his career, his effectiveness, and his self-esteem.

Like many of my clients, Tom's problem wasn't the tasks associated with his job; it was his relationship with someone at work.

▣ THE #1 SOURCE OF STRESS

Most stress in the workplace today is not the *functional stress* of difficult tasks, deadlines, and other common on-the-job challenges, but the *interpersonal stress* of problems with other people: bosses, coworkers, and staff.

Many of my clients have a Jack (or Jacqueline) in their lives—someone around whom they just can't seem to win, or with whom they have trouble communicating. Sometimes the whole atmosphere in the office is so stressful that people feel thwarted when they try to do a good job or to work productively and supportively with others. My clients often say they have the baffling, disquieting feeling that they aren't even acting like themselves, that somehow they have time-warped back into the past and are behaving as they did when they were children—or worse, behaving as their parents behaved.

Some of these people struggle to please oppressive bosses, working unreasonable hours and complaining only to friends, relatives, and coworkers—never to the boss. Others waste time and energy combating competitive coworkers' power plays or wrestling with managers' mixed messages. Still others have trouble motivating their staffs and beat themselves up for resorting to coercion when their attempts at honesty and direct communication don't seem to work.

My clients may be wearing business clothes and earning adult salaries, but on the job they feel they might as well be in short pants and knee socks—or torn jeans and high tops if they are twenty- or thirty-somethings.

They are angry and confused. Grinding their emotional wheels on interpersonal problems keeps them from focusing on their jobs, getting ahead, having fun, and feeling good about themselves. It is a frustrating waste of time, money, energy, and talent.

▣ MYSTERIOUS MALAISE

What's really going on when you do your job well and make decent money but you don't get the raises and promotions you want? Why is it that you can hardly stand to drag yourself to work each morning? What forces are at work when:

- You feel beaten up, discouraged, or vaguely angry at the end of the day but can't point to anything specific that made you feel that way?

- You feel nervous, power-tripped, or manipulated around certain people but can never pinpoint why?

- You get stuck in no-win situations that keep you from doing your job well and make you look bad?

- You have to speak or act in ways that feel unnatural, petty, or dishonest and can't talk about what's really going on?

- You just don't feel heard, respected, or acknowledged for what you do?

If you've had any of these experiences, you are not alone. Yet few people in corporate offices talk openly about these problems, and the whispers and gossip aren't very productive. No one seems to know just how professional relationships really work, where they go off course, and what you can do to get them back on track.

The problem isn't simply cruel or inept bosses, lazy or incompetent staffs, critical or negative coworkers. Those people are out there, but heaping all the blame on them robs you of your power to change and improve the situation. It also ignores what may be the most important factor in difficult work relationships—the missing piece that explains why these associations feel so stressful, and yet so familiar.

▣ STOWAWAYS IN YOUR BRIEFCASE

I believe that the key to having productive, supportive, and enjoyable relationships with people at work is understanding that the emotional dynamics of a workplace as a whole often resemble the emotional dynamics of a family. Moreover, when we are under stress, we tend to revert to the coping strategies we learned as children.

When we have trouble at work, it's often because we find ourselves in crucial situations feeling—and often acting and talking—like eight-year-olds relating to overbearing fathers, guilt-tripping mothers, teasing older brothers, or competitive younger sisters. The problem is that we aren't eight anymore, and the people we encounter at work are *not* our fathers, mothers, and siblings. The strategies we used as children are no longer appropriate, useful, effective, or healthy.

These strategies are part of the *family patterns* that develop in every family. I'll be using this phrase throughout the book to describe the coping mechanisms that people learned in their families under stress, and for which they grasp instinctively when relationships at work become difficult.

FAMILY PATTERNS

Family patterns are repeated sets of behaviors and rules that family members use to interact with each other and maintain the family system.

Whenever people come together in groups, they tend to re-create the emotional dynamics of families. People who work together may be the most likely kind of group to become a "family." We see one another almost every day and spend long periods of time together. To some extent, our emotional well-being and economic security are dependent on one another.

Not all the attitudes and behaviors we learned in our families are unhealthy. Our parents may also have taught us productive, caring ways of relating to others. Unfortunately, it's more often the unhealthy behaviors that come to work because, as we'll explore in the following chapter, those are the ones designed to cover up stressful feelings and maintain control—important ingredients in most corporate environments.

It's only natural that we would revert unconsciously to these defensive behaviors when we feel tense or frustrated. They were the first things we learned about dealing with other people, and we may have spent years practicing them. No matter how ineffective, or even painful, they may be, we fall into them automatically because they are familiar.

▣ PLAYING DEFENSE: FAMILY STRATEGIES

These defensive patterns of thinking, relating, and behaving probably helped us through some difficult emotional situations when we were very young, and if we thought of them at all, we might think of them as emotional survival tools.

When we're children and terrified of losing Dad's attention or Mom's love, we'll do whatever it takes to feel secure again—including using our dirtiest tricks and most manipulative tactics. When we find ourselves threatened by difficult or stressful relationships today, these old behaviors can kick in before we know what hit us.

It's no accident that Tom felt like a kid around his boss Jack, particularly when his desire for Jack's approval was thwarted. He did exactly what he'd done when his father bawled him out for not getting A's or made him come home by ten o'clock on weekends. He rebelled, acted out, and sulked. These behaviors are more dangerous now than they were when Tom was a child and adolescent. Back then, he was grounded or scolded. Now, they can cost him raises, promotions, and possibly his job.

Here are some other ways that people can revert automatically to old family patterns of thinking, acting, and relating:

- Norman, a CEO facing a disastrous third quarter, instinctively withheld the bad news as long as possible from people who needed to know, but who might punish him for his poor performance.

- Becky, an ad-agency account exec, encountered loud resistance from male colleagues when she tried to set production deadlines. She unconsciously followed her family's rule that women exist to support men and make them happy, and backed down with an apologetic smile.

- Greg didn't feel that his boss Louise was giving him enough credit or attention, but he didn't want to say that to her directly. Instead, he started making mistakes and causing trouble. It got Louise's attention, just as it had gotten his mother's attention when he was a child, but it didn't do his performance evaluation any good.

- When a scandal exploded around the mayor, his assistant Cheryl made matters worse by trying to handle everything single-handedly—the media, the horrified staff, and angry party officials—just as she had tried to hold her family together single-handedly as the oldest daughter when her mother got drunk.

▣ YOU CAN ONLY CLAIM YOUR OWN BAGGAGE

As I mentioned in the Introduction, families and organizations are both emotional systems in which everybody's thoughts, feelings, and actions affect one another and are mutually interdependent. How Henry interprets Judy's smile—is it encouraging or smug?—can easily affect his next interaction with Len, who is then in a bad mood when he runs into Judy because Henry yelled at him. This is why the model of family systems therapy, which treats relationships among individuals as part of an emotional web or system, is a useful approach to work relationships as well.

FAMILY SYSTEMS THERAPY

Family systems therapy views the problems of individual family members as a function of the behavior and communication patterns of the whole family. In addition, the family is examined as a system in which each member's thoughts, feelings and behavior influence the other member's.

Because your workplace is a system that includes everybody's family patterns, some of the emotional baggage there is yours, and other patterns were in place long before you arrived.

It can be uncomfortable to identify your own baggage, as you'll do in Part 2 of this book, but that is where your power lies. You can only change what's yours. Trying to change other people can be fruitless and frustrating, so even though you may be surrounded at work by other people's abrasive, distressing family patterns, you'll be concentrating in this book on finding *your* baggage.

◨ "B U T   W E   D I D   I T   A L L   F O R   Y O U . . ."

Some people have trouble accepting that family patterns of behavior play such a key role in their relationships at work. There are several reasons for this:

1. *It is hard to believe that we're still influenced by events that took place twenty, thirty, or forty years ago.* We forget how formative those early experiences were, and we've given many childlike behaviors a very adult disguise. Manipulation can look powerful, rebellion can appear to be standing up for yourself, and sullen withdrawal can wear the mask of objectivity.

2. *It feels disloyal, unfair, or ungrateful to blame our parents or siblings for our present situation.* It's important to remember that this process is not about finding fault or assigning blame; it is about recognizing patterns that we have adopted, seeing what they cost us, and taking positive steps to change them.

3. *Talking about difficult feelings and family issues can be desperately uncomfortable.* Family is a vulnerable area, for better or worse, for almost everyone. It's much easier to hide behind the traditional corporate work ethic of putting your feelings aside and just getting the job done.

It's not always easy or pleasant to look closely at family dynamics, but that's the key to coming to terms with difficult work relationships.

When you understand your own family patterns—the ways of think-ing, relating, and behaving that you are most likely to bring to work—then you are no longer at the mercy of habitual childlike emotional responses. You're better able to pull back from those behaviors and make choices based on the present rather than the past.

◘ TIES THAT BIND

Falling back on unhealthy, defensive behaviors you learned as a child can be costly—emotionally, financially, and even physically. Obviously, it's not ideal to relate to people at work as if you were a child or to treat coworkers the way your parents treated you, but these interactions have some hidden costs as well:

- *You are less productive.* Troubled relationships are exhausting and cause what little energy you have left to be focused on other people rather than on your job. People in my organizational seminars—from corporation presidents to part-time clerks in corner stores—estimate that they lose *20–50 percent of their productive work time* to emotional conflicts with others.

- *You are more susceptible to anxiety, frustration, hurt, and anger; you feel powerless.* These feelings not only lower self-esteem but also make you less effective.

- *It's harder to feel accepted, recognized, and fulfilled.* Without a sense of accomplishment, enthusiasm, and loyalty—to the organization, the work group, or even to yourself—you're just going through the mo-tions. That's no fun and gets you nowhere.

- *You're more likely to burn out or encounter stress-related conditions.* These include depression, headaches, insomnia, ulcers, fatigue, and dependence on alcohol, food, or other substances and behavior.

- *You feel tight, constrained, and emotionally stifled.* Most of the un-healthy behaviors that find their way to work were developed to sup-press uncomfortable feelings or cover up conflicts. It is just as unhealthy to avoid problems and repress emotions at work as it is to stuff them at home.

Many people feel discouraged, even hopeless, in the face of all these difficulties. What do you do when relationships feel so incapable of change, so hurtful or debilitating, so manipulative and even dangerous that there seems to be no way out? You may think you have only three options:

* Quit.

* Ignore the difficult relationship and your feelings about it, and try to put up with the debilitating stress.

* Take the problem underground into a stressful, murky world of gossip and alliances that sets up an "us against them" mentality, and ultimately only makes you feel even worse.

None of these options is really acceptable—nor is succumbing to the temptation to throw pencil sharpeners, trash files, power-drill hard disks, cram paper clips into A-drives, or pour molasses into fax machines. There are other, healthier, more pleasant, and more productive alternatives.

▣ FROM SURVIVING TO THRIVING

Some people are satisfied to survive at work. They may earn advanced degrees and take seminars to improve their skills, but they don't feel happy, enthusiastic, or in control. They don't understand that work relationships can generate stress and low self-esteem, that they may be reinforcing old patterns that make them feel even more stressed and powerless, or that there is anything they can do about it. They may even appear to be climbing the professional ladder successfully, but they rarely experience much joy, confidence, or fulfillment.

Thriving at work is something entirely different. It is a *proactive* response based on taking charge of your experience in work relationships, looking for your part in situations, and taking the initiative to resolve problems and relieve stress. Instead of merely reacting to people and situations, you examine your own thoughts, feelings, and actions—and you understand that you have choices about how you relate to others.

Thriving at work requires a commitment to yourself and to your own happiness and satisfaction. It does mean being willing to examine and change behaviors that have become unhealthy habits, but it generates enormous self-esteem and personal power—both on and off the job.

▣ USING THIS BOOK FOR CHANGE

Making changes in your work relationships can be challenging, richly rewarding—and risky. You will be stirring up an organization that may be structured along rigid hierarchical lines, as many families are. That organization, and the people in it, may turn on you unless you proceed with caution and a well-planned strategy.

I strongly suggest that you do not try introducing changes at work until you have finished reading this book and doing all the exercises in it. Your situation is unique. You need to uncover information and plan strategies specific to your office or corporation in order to avoid unnecessary upset and putting your job at risk.

In difficult times, you may not have the option of quitting your job, any more than you could quit your family—yet the same stressful economic factors that make it prudent for you to stay may also trigger problems in relationships at work. The good news is that by staying and working through these difficult situations, you won't re-create them again when you have more mobility and can leave. You'll be able to walk into any job, at any company, with the tools to make your relationships there work.

Making changes takes courage. It means giving up the idea that there is nothing you can do and taking a stand for yourself. The rewards are healthy, productive, and fulfilling relationships with bosses, coworkers, and staff. You can take control of your own destiny, and need never feel powerless around these people again.

2

Why Your Boss Looks Like Your Mother

Why do we do it? We know it's not smart or fun to act like children at work or to treat others like children. Yet once you're aware of the tendency to bring your family's emotional patterns to the office, you see it everywhere.

How do these behaviors travel through time and space to pop up at the most inappropriate moments—both in everyday situations and on such crucial occasions as salary reviews, performance evaluations, and interviews for promotions?

Your company may actually encourage these behaviors. Most organizations do. Five conditions exist in almost every workplace that foster these old, unproductive ways of thinking and acting—and keep them in place. This chapter examines those five conditions. Understanding what triggers and sustains family patterns at work is the first step in learning to short-circuit them.

WHY WORK ENVIRONMENTS ENCOURAGE FAMILY PATTERNS: THE FIVE CONDITIONS

1. The workplace is a breeding ground for stress.

2. In the workplace, emotional desires are often thwarted.

3. The expression of feelings has no place at work.

4. The invisible world is a fact of corporate life.

5. In the corporate pinball game, everyone bounces off everyone else.

◻ BARBARA'S STORY

Barbara was an artist at a design firm. She loved her work and was doing quite well until the firm landed an important cereal account and hired another artist, Jason, to help with the increased work load. Suddenly, Barbara had two new sources of stress in her life. First, everyone was working day and night on the new cereal ads. Second, she quickly saw that Jason was much faster and more innovative than she was, and his obvious superiority was deflating and threatening. Barbara became consumed with jealousy, fear, and anger. She was embarrassed to feel these emotions and tried desperately to hide them from people in the office—at least at first.

Nicole, another artist in the department, commiserated with Barbara and agreed that Jason wasn't all *that* good at what he did, that he acted affected and superior, and that he probably was favored by Amanda, their departmental head. Their alliance against Jason stirred up hostile undercurrents that were felt throughout the firm but never discussed openly.

As the deadline for the first cereal ads approached and Jason looked even more like a star, Barbara's campaign against him intensified. Barbara convinced Nicole, her ally, to tell Amanda how disruptive Jason was, how department morale had plummeted since his arrival, and how they'd all be happier and get more done if he weren't around. But when Nicole said as much to their boss, Amanda took a stand. She told Nicole that if there were staff cuts, only team players would stay. Nicole got the message. Gradually, she pulled away from Barbara and made peace with Jason.

Barbara found herself alone, feeling angry, frustrated, and secretly afraid. She hated going to work each morning and began to suffer from asthma and severe headaches. She hadn't experienced this combination of symptoms since she was a child, and it was this red flag that alerted her to the fact that something was very wrong. It brought her both to a physician and to me.

Barbara's story illustrates the five conditions in every workplace that encourage the defensive patterns of behavior we learned in our families.

▣ CONDITION #1: THE WORKPLACE IS A BREEDING GROUND FOR STRESS

Every workplace has two volatile ingredients that combine to produce a stress-filled environment in which such survival tactics as intimidation, sullen withdrawal, emotional triangles, covert competition, perfectionism, rebellion, and manipulation by martyrdom can grow and flourish. These two factors exacerbate one another.

1. *Work is a functionally stressful place.* Tasks have to get done, deadlines have to be met, and your economic survival may depend on keeping your job. Every position has at least some functional stress, even if it's only the stress of showing up for work on time.

2. *We are all different from one another and bring different sets of emotional baggage to work.* We all have different family backgrounds and learned in childhood to deal with other people in different ways. We have different needs and see life from slightly different points of view. Often these points of view and strategies for relating are in conflict with other people's viewpoints and tactics. We may pick friends or mates with whom our views and strategies don't conflict, but in

an office we can't always make those choices. We work with the people who are there, whether or not we see the world (and how to communicate in that world) the same way.

The more conflict there is between your outlook and another person's, the more potential for stress there is in that relationship.

Under stress, we tend to fall back into the patterns of relating that we learned in our families. We don't always *act* on this tendency to relate to people at work as the people in our families related to one another, but those emotional survival strategies are etched in our minds. They will always be our first, instinctive reaction to stress, and we can only reverse them through conscious effort. Old habits die hard. We walk in the office door with a predisposition to relate to Mary on the support staff as we did to Aunt Helen, or to the boss as we did to an overbearing father, or to a colleague as we did to a pesky younger sister. All it takes to trigger these old habits is a little extra tension or conflict, as Barbara felt when the firm landed the cereal account and Jason came on board.

In our work together, Barbara realized that she had been reacting to Jason as she had reacted to her handsome, smart, popular, athletic, and "perfect" older brother. The only way she'd been able to get attention from her parents or other siblings was to form emotional triangles and competitive alliances with them against him. She would try to get him into trouble by saying that he was the one who had spilled the soda, broken the doll, thrown the baseball that broke the window—whether or not he had actually done these things. If he looked bad, she somehow felt she looked better in comparison, especially if one of the others in her family sided with her against him. Even when no one believed her, at least she was the center of attention for a moment, the focal point of a dramatic conflict.

EMOTIONAL TRIANGLES

An emotional triangle forms when Person A attempts to alleviate interpersonal stress in his or her relationship with Person B by forming an emotional alliance with Person C.

It was a strategy Barbara had learned from her parents and watched everyone in her family use. If you felt someone else was getting your share of the attention, acknowledgment, or love, you simply tried to turn the others against him. You grabbed a white hat for yourself, tried to gather a posse of other family members around you, and went after the bad guy. Even if you didn't catch him, you created a lot of dust and noise. At least everybody noticed you for a change. Although she appeared to be grown up on the outside, at work Barbara's instinctive reaction to being second best when Jason became a star was to grab an ally, Nicole, and try to turn everyone else against him.

Every workplace is a fertile breeding ground for family patterns because the normal stress of getting tasks done both reveals our differences and triggers our tendency to grasp at old defensive strategies.

▣ CONDITION #2: IN THE WORKPLACE, EMOTIONAL DESIRES ARE OFTEN THWARTED

Most companies don't want to talk about them, and few people know exactly what they are, but we all have three fundamental emotional desires that must be met at work. A paycheck isn't enough for most of us; we need to feel a basic level of self-esteem. In Chapter 13, you will analyze whether your emotional desires are being met—by the people you want to meet them—in your particular situation. That exercise will be a key tool in deciding what you want to change.

Will Schutz, a human relations consultant and author of *The Truth Option,* first identified these desires, which I paraphrase as follows:

- We want to feel *included* and *recognized.*

- We want to feel *competent* and *in control* of our jobs.

- We want to feel *accepted* and *liked* by others.

When these desires are thwarted—or even when we think they might be thwarted—we are likely to feel angry, hurt, disappointed, sad, afraid, frustrated, jealous, rejected, resentful, or ashamed. No job can satisfy all of our desires, all of the time, so we often feel some uncomfortable emotions. To cope with these uneasy feelings, we often gravitate unconsciously toward the tactics our families used to deal with uncomfortable relationships.

When Jason appeared on the scene, all three of Barbara's basic emotional desires were threatened, and she panicked. He was faster and appeared to be more creative than she was, so she no longer felt as *competent*. She didn't feel her work was *recognized*. With all the tension and animosity in the office, she no longer felt *liked* or *accepted* by others.

When her emotional desires were thwarted—and looked as if they might be thwarted further—she felt angry, frightened, and frustrated. Instinctively, she tried doing what people in her family had done when they felt angry or frightened. They formed emotional triangles and beat up on the third party. For thirty years, Barbara had been repeating this pattern without even being aware of it.

▣ CONDITION #3: THE EXPRESSION OF FEELINGS HAS NO PLACE AT WORK

I believe American corporations have an unwritten rule that's virtually guaranteed to bring ineffective family-learned emotional strategies to the surface—often in explosive, surprising, and overwhelming ways.

Most of my clients report that in their organizations there is a powerful, unspoken taboo against expressing, or even having, negative feelings—especially such uncomfortable feelings as anger, hurt, resentment, disappointment, sadness, fear, frustration, jealousy, shame, confusion, or rejection. Positive feelings may be tolerated or even encouraged because they suggest high motivation or excitement, but there are no structures within many companies for handling difficult, uncomfortable emotions.

The message most employers send, explicitly or implicitly, is: *Feelings have no place at work; they just interfere with getting the job done.* The idea is that work is different from life and that uncomfortable emotions don't exist at work.

If we were robots, this system would work perfectly. We would all line up in our little cubes on the organizational chart, do our work, collect our paychecks, and go home. The problem is, we are human beings and we take our human, feeling selves with us wherever we go—even to work.

When we can't deal with our emotions as adults, acknowledging them and speaking of them directly, then we're more likely to act them out, often as we did when we were children. Those feelings don't go away just because we can't express them. They go underground, grow, and fester until finally they explode out of control in ways that are often unhealthy and unproductive—usually in the form of primal, instinctive behaviors that we learned when we were young.

We often resort to old childhood behaviors when we have to stifle our uncomfortable emotions for two reasons. First, it's stressful to deny or ignore feelings. As stressful as having those difficult feelings may be, it is even more stressful to suppress them. And second, having to suppress our feelings reminds us of home, and we fall back into old ways of thinking and behaving. Negative feelings weren't acceptable in most of our families, either. We weren't supposed to feel angry at one another, or hurt by one another, or even disappointed with a birthday present. Even if we felt those things, we weren't supposed to talk about them. The family had to look happy and perfect at all times. Anything less represented a threat to its survival or reputation.

In fact, most families' unhealthy ways of relating to one another are specifically designed to avoid or mask these "dangerous" emotions so that the family looks good, people don't feel as uncomfortable, and stress is kept to a minimum. It doesn't work, of course. Suppressing emotions just makes them more intense, creates more stress, and causes more discomfort—but that doesn't stop people from trying.

Two-against-one emotional triangles can be efforts to dull the pain of rejection, loneliness, shame, or hurt. Sulking or rebelling are often attempts to avoid frustration, sadness, or disappointment. Covert power games, intimidation, or scapegoating can temporarily cover up fear or jealousy. Silent withdrawal can mask anger. (Particular behaviors don't necessarily match up with specific feelings. In Chapter 12, you will assess which patterns your family used to mask which emotions.)

21

Barbara didn't look at herself in the mirror every morning before going off to the design firm and say, "Today I think I'll put my job and health at risk by creating an emotional triangle at work." She felt frustrated and frightened, and slid unconsciously into her habitual defense against those feelings. It never occurred to her that she could choose a different response. Expressing feelings was considered unprofessional at Barbara's firm, and so nothing at work encouraged her to examine the feelings this habit was designed to cover up. The emotional environment at work actually encouraged her to suppress her feelings and resort to old, defensive behaviors.

The problem wasn't that she had learned an unproductive strategy for coping with stress as a child—that's part of being human—but that she fell into it automatically and unconsciously, and so *she had no control over it.*

For Barbara, forming competitive alliances and triangles was as natural as breathing. If someone had pointed out to her what she was doing, she probably would have said, "What's wrong with confiding in my peers? And my boss should know about this guy!" Maybe so, if Jason had been embezzling money from the company. But in this case his disruptive behavior was only in Barbara's mind.

When we routinely deny or ignore our emotions at work, eventually we get confused. We don't understand why we feel tired all the time, or depressed, or why we have chronic flu symptoms, or are bored by our jobs, or can't stand to deal with people at work. We don't recognize that these are all symptoms of getting emotionally clogged.

◙ CONDITION #4: THE INVISIBLE WORLD IS A FACT OF CORPORATE LIFE

If you've ever felt that things happen in your office that you can't talk about, or that what really goes on inside your organization is different from how it appears on the outside, then you've experienced the invisible world.

The invisible world is the sum total of everything you can't talk about directly or publicly, the secret reality behind the corporate masks, the shadowy world of stifled feelings and hidden information, ambiguous or troubled relationships, unacknowledged connections among people, office politics, corporate lies, and private gossip. The invisible world can become the organization's driving force, fostering a wide variety of sticky situations:

- A computer firm is written up in business magazines for its free-wheeling management style, relaxed dress code, and flexible hours—but everybody who works there knows it's just as much a hotbed of office politics as the low-tech, old-fashioned, uptight company next door.

- Sandra would like her sales manager Ken to ask her out. He knows this and uses it to get her to produce more sales. He even talks up her coworker Lori to create a competitive situation between them for his personal and professional attention. Ken gets ego strokes and fantastic results in his department. His game happens to be helping, or at least not hurting, Sandra's career—but she's not getting what she wants, she's not happy, and she's not being treated with honesty or respect.

- The support staff at a management consulting firm are constantly being scapegoated for problems that clients have with delivery of reports. At the same time the staff knows they must maintain a positive outlook and avoid talking about what's really going on: high turnover in junior consultants, broken promises about merit increases, and the growing tension between two vice presidents.

- At a large investment company, unwelcome flirtations and even physical advances go unreported because people know that management doesn't believe there's any such thing as sexual harassment.

Whatever the invisible world in your office looks like, it is probably quite different from the face your organization shows the world. The visible, public reality in most companies is made up of organizational charts, policy statements, procedures manuals, annual reports, and budgets. It is a hierarchy of clear, precise relationships and functions that can be written down and talked about—a glossy world of high-minded policies and neatly defined job descriptions.

In the organization's visible world, people are all focused on being productive and working as a team. Everyone is supposed to be happy, and nobody feels anything negative. The visible, external structures imposed by corporations are designed to give people certainty about what is going on and to make the organization run efficiently and effectively, but often management ignores emotional realities and has little connection to what people are actually feeling and thinking.

The difference between the visible and invisible worlds can be seen most clearly in the three dynamics that govern how people interact with one another:

* *Roles* tell us who we are within the group.

* *Rules* tell us what we can and cannot do and say.

* *Ways of relating* tell us how to interact with other group members.

An organization's visible roles, rules, and ways of relating dictate how people are supposed to interact with one another, while the invisible roles, rules, and ways of relating—based on thoughts and emotions—reflect how people actually do interact.

Recognizing the difference between your company's invisible world and its visible world is an essential element in improving your relationships with people at work. In Part 2, you will explore similarities between your company's invisible world and the invisible roles, rules, and ways of relating that existed in your family. That connection is the key to making the changes you'll implement in Part 3.

Roles

The visible roles in your organization are the job titles: CEO, vice president, personnel director, corporate communications manager, support staff, and so on.

In the invisible reality, however, people may act out more emotionally based roles that they learned in their families: Superachievers, Martyrs, Victims, Heroes, Rebels, Rescuers, Caretakers, Scapegoats, "Bad" Children, Quiet "Good" Children, Mascots, Clowns, Persecutors, Tyrants, Cheerleaders, or People Pleasers. These roles are the basic ones that have been identified over the past twenty years both in family therapy literature and in the field of addiction recovery. People are, of course, complex, and we are far more than a stereotyped set of dominant behaviors. Nonetheless, we do often behave in similar, categorizable ways, each role fairly consistent and recognizable.

- Gene's visible role is CEO, but everybody knows he's just a weak, wimpy People Pleaser whom the board appointed to be a rubber stamp.

- Virginia is a counselor in the Human Resources Division, but nobody goes to her because they know that in the invisible reality, she's a Martyr who complains about having to listen to people's problems all day.

Rules

Your organization's visible rules deal with logistics, getting things done, and what people can and cannot do. They tell you things like what time to be at work in the morning, how often performance reviews occur, when expense reports must be submitted, and what the penalties are for infractions. Most people follow these rules, or they don't stay in the organization.

It's the invisible rules that cause confusion and stress. They are unstated, unwritten, and often people deny that they exist—but people who violate them can find themselves in serious trouble. Some common invisible rules are:

- Pretend you're happy with your job, coworkers, and boss—even if you're not.

- Make the boss look good, even if it makes you look bad.

- Act like you know what you're doing, even if you don't.

- Protect management from anything negative, no matter what.

- Getting the work done is more important than your mental or physical health.

- Loyalty is the most important thing. Don't question the company's methods or authority, even if what it says doesn't make sense.

- If you're not happy about the rules here, leave.

These invisible rules are often at odds with visible company policy:

- The CEO says his door is always open and he wants people's input, but the last two people who voiced complaints found themselves transferred to the Nome office. The *visible* policy is to let management know if you have a problem; the *invisible* reality is that if you cross the CEO, he'll put as much distance as possible between you and him.

- The organization prides itself on the number of women executives, but none of them ever seem to make it to the vice presidential level. The *visible* policy is equal opportunity; the *invisible* reality is a glass ceiling.

Ways of Relating

Your organization's visible aspirations for how people should relate to one another may include open communication, employee support, staff recognition, and conflict resolution through negotiation. Sometimes these aspirations are achieved, but more often they are either replaced by or mixed with the invisible, more manipulative ways of relating that people bring to the office from their families: competition, denial or avoidance, emotional triangles, mixed messages, covert power games, silent withdrawal, attacking or bullying, bribing, placating, coercion by martyrdom, blaming, shaming, criticizing, intimidation, domination, patronizing, threats, and verbal abuse.

These invisible dynamics are often known as office politics. Here are two examples:

- The Human Resources Department has a staff mediator to help resolve conflicts among people at different levels in the company, but Frank didn't use the service when he had trouble with his staff. Being labeled as a problematic boss might have hurt his chances for promotion. The *visible* policy was resolving conflicts by negotiation; the *invisible* way of relating was gossip. Frank knew that word about him would travel through the grapevine to people who could damage his career.

- Mutual respect and open communication receive lip service at staff meetings, but Paula knows that her boss Phyllis is more likely to employ quiet intimidation—and that if their work group doesn't placate and appease her, she will carry out her subtle threats.

The invisible world exists in every workplace, side by side with your company's visible structures—and having to live in both worlds can be stressful. Trying to do your job with one foot in one world and the other foot in another can demand your attention, sap your energy, undermine your effectiveness, and prompt you to deal with the people at work using the same interpersonal skills you had when you were five years old.

You have to get dressed, go to the office, and play your part in the visible reality every day, but you can never escape the invisible world of feelings and relationships. You may have to treat your boss as if he's more competent than he actually is and work hard to make him look good, for example, but you may also feel angry or resentful as a result—and be tempted to react in the same ways you learned to deal with anger and resentment as a child.

We can't escape the invisible world, but we can learn to understand it better and to deal with our reactions in more effective ways. You'll begin that process in Part 2.

◙ CONDITION #5: IN THE CORPORATE PINBALL GAME, EVERYONE BOUNCES OFF EVERYONE ELSE

Nobody operates in a vacuum. Emotional exchanges take place in all human relationships, even when they are ignored, invalidated, or denied. They occur whether we are having an informal conversation, overhauling a transmission, or formulating a marketing strategy. We all bring our childhoods to work with us, and all of our moods, feelings, thoughts, behaviors, and expectations continually influence one another.

Some people have more emotional impact on you than others. Your boss or someone you care about may have more influence over you than someone you hardly know or whose work has no relationship to yours. The more emotional impact a person has on you, the greater the potential for stress in your relationship with that person—and so the more likely you are to fall back on old emotional tactics that were used in your family.

It's inevitable that when one person starts applying the tactics that he or she used to manipulate others at age six, it will trigger the defensive tactics that someone else used at age seven. Since these strategies are not likely to make anyone else in the office feel particularly safe, respected, or liked, their behaviors will trigger everyone else's old family dynamics until the whole organization begins to resemble a giant game of emotional pinball. Lights start to flash. Bells and whistles go off. Shiny balls bounce up, down, and around against unpredictable obstacles. It can be exciting, but in the end, nothing gets done. Pinball is fine for recreation, but it's no way to run your career or manage your emotional well-being.

Every organization has an ongoing, large-scale intramural pinball game. It is the sum total of everybody's emotional impact on everybody else, the composite of everyone's feelings, mutual reactions, relationships, and intermingling family behaviors. Everybody is a player, whether or not he chooses to participate or even knows he's in the game.

▣ THE STRESS EXPRESS

Think about the extraordinary stress involved when all five of these conditions exist simultaneously, as they do in many organizations.

1. The natural stresses of any office set off our tendency to react to people at work.

2. Everybody in this environment has unspoken emotional desires that, when thwarted, result in stressful feelings that trigger more family behaviors.

3. We aren't supposed to have feelings at work, but we have them anyway. Our relationships with bosses, coworkers, and staff are filled with emotions, especially if work is important to us. When those feelings are denied or suppressed, they go underground and fester until finally they explode in the form of behaviors we used to cope when we were children.

4. These suppressed feelings, unacknowledged relationships, and family behaviors coalesce into an invisible world with its own set of roles, rules, and ways of relating. The invisible world runs on emotions and powers the organization, but it can't be acknowledged or discussed—and therefore nothing in it can be resolved.

5. The pinball game begins. All of these unspoken emotional undercurrents and old family behaviors start triggering one another and ricocheting off one another until there is so much emotional noise that it's difficult to know what's happening or what to do about it.

Some people get so hopeless about this process, so overwhelmed by the bells and whistles, that they throw up their hands and say, "That's just the way it is. Live with it!" I say that you can't eliminate the stress of the workplace or your tendency to react, but you can take specific, positive steps to turn around stressful relationships and build a healthy emotional environment in your office.

First, though, you must learn to recognize your own part in the drama. How can you tell when you're reacting defensively with the tactics you learned as a child and when your response is appropriate and adult? Part 2 gives you the tools to make this distinction and to ease even the most difficult situations.

Part Two

YOUR BOSS OR YOUR MOTHER: WHAT FAMILY PATTERNS DO YOU BRING TO WORK?

In Part 1, we looked at what family patterns are and how they function. Part 2 is about *you*—your office and your family. You'll explore the various roles, rules, and ways of relating that you learned in your family; identify when you slip into these patterns; and discover some general techniques for lessening the stress in your relationships.

As we've noted, there are two parts to any difficult work situation: the dynamics that were in place before you arrived and the emotional baggage that you brought with you from your family. You can only change what you brought with you, so it's important to know what your own baggage looks like. You'll use this information in Part 3 to decide what changes you want to make, and how best to make them without jeopardizing your job.

Chapter 3 shows you how to tell when you've slipped into one of your own family patterns. Chapters 4–6 explore more deeply the invisible family roles that you may bring to work. You'll identify how you may play different roles depending on the situation and the people with whom you are interacting.

In Chapter 7, you'll look at how you learned to react to invisible rules and mixed messages in your family and see if you're bringing some of those same behaviors to work today.

Chapter 8 and Chapter 9 explore the most common invisible ways of relating that we learned in our families. Chapter 10 offers techniques you can use to empower yourself in difficult relationships even before you start making specific changes.

As you read about invisible roles, rules, and ways of relating in Chapters 4–9, think about which of these dynamics engage you most strongly. What emotional roles do you play at work, perhaps without being aware of it? Were these roles you played in your family? Do any of the unwritten rules at work remind you of unstated rules in your family? How do you react to them? Have you brought any of your family's unproductive ways of relating to the office?

◩ You may be surprised, as many of my clients are, to see how closely situations at the office resemble those that occurred in families. It often seems uncanny that someone with a bossy, competitive older sister and a martyred mother will later find herself in a work situation with a bossy, competitive colleague and a martyred boss—and have some of the same reactions that she had when she was a child.

The emotional patterns that dominate our work lives are so remarkably similar to those that dominated our families for two reasons:

1. A person who grew up with a particular dynamic will tend to *perceive* that dynamic, even when it is weak or perhaps not even present. If Sharon's father was demanding and judgmental, for instance, she might perceive Craig as an "oppressive" boss even though others (who didn't grow up with demanding fathers) don't see Craig that way at all.

2. The dynamics that trigger us, capture our attention, and make us react are the ones that we felt threatened us emotionally when we were young, vulnerable, and easily frightened. If there are thirty different unproductive behaviors going on in Sharon's office, she'll ignore the rest and focus on Craig's "oppression."

Part 2 is about understanding your unique situation, learning skills that promote supportive work relationships even before you make specific changes, and gathering the information you'll use in Part 3 to take charge and make changes.

3

Seven Red Flags: Recognizing Your Own Family-Patterned Reactions

How can you tell if you've slipped into unproductive emotional tactics you learned as a child, or if you're simply responding normally to a difficult situation?

When your boss gives you only the minimum salary increase and you get furious, for example, are you throwing a childish tantrum or simply responding appropriately as a mistreated adult? When you feel ignored and try to get your boss's attention, are you struggling to make a parent notice you or just being professionally assertive?

The distinction between family-learned reactions and natural adult responses can be confusing at first, especially since family patterns surface in stressful situations, when we may not be thinking as clearly as we normally do.

In this chapter, I'll show you how to recognize when you're firing weapons from your family's emotional-survival arsenal. With practice, you'll become adept at spotting these behaviors and be able to stop before you escalate the situation with knee-jerk reactions. You will begin to notice that certain kinds of people or situations repeatedly trigger certain uncomfortable feelings in you—anger, fear, resentment, and so on—and that these feelings trigger specific defensive reactions, such as silence and emotional withdrawal, rebellion, martyrdom, or some other invisible role, rule, or way of relating that you learned in your family.

As you become aware of what your particular patterns and triggers are, you'll have a road map showing your own individual potholes so that you can begin to avoid them. You can also use this information to complete the exercises in Part 3 and decide what changes you want to make.

In my practice, I've found seven red flags that indicate you are using an old family tactic for dealing with stress and conflict—or that you're about to do so.

▣ RED FLAG #1: YOU REPEAT REACTIONS AND CONFLICTS

Repetition is the primary warning sign and distinguishing characteristic of family-learned emotional defenses. If you find yourself losing the same battles again and again, you may well be fighting an enemy from your past—and sabotaging your present in the process.

• Steve couldn't believe it when, once again, a coworker to whom he'd been particularly helpful was promoted over him. On his last two jobs, he had been the likable good guy who helped everybody get ahead—except himself. The third time this happened, he came to me.

• After Pamela's new boss asked her for some additions and corrections to a report, she found herself crying in the restroom, feeling victimized and beaten down. She realized that this was just how she had reacted when her old boss asked for even minor changes.

When you feel stuck in a rut, always reacting the same way to certain kinds of people or situations, you are probably defending yourself with an emotional dynamic that you learned in your family.

If you always seem to be cast in one particular role—Superachiever, Rebel, or Tyrant, for example—at job after job, ask yourself if that was a role you often played as a child. If you always feel like a Victim with bosses, coworkers, or even staff, consider whether you often felt like a Victim in your family.

If you are often involved in the same kind of arguments—loud and violent ones, quiet but venomous ones, sarcastic or convoluted ones— examine whether that's how arguments were conducted in your family. If the boss always seems to prefer someone else to you and you have the same reaction over and over—you withdraw or rebel, for example—check to see if that was how you attempted to get your parents' attention.

Whenever you notice that you are repeating a reaction or conflict, stop and consider: Did you play out that same pattern of behavior with the people in your family?

It isn't always easy to recognize these patterns at first. It takes practice and commitment, but it becomes more natural as you begin to experience the benefits of better relationships with people at work.

▣ RED FLAG #2: YOU BLAME OR OBSESS ABOUT OTHERS

When you first start looking for family patterns, you may see other people's faults and defensive behaviors more clearly than your own. It may seem that all your problems are caused by an overbearing or ineffective boss, mean-spirited coworkers, or lazy staff people who are stuck in *their* family patterns.

This is a natural reaction. Blaming is one of the most common strategies for emotional survival in families; if you habitually lay the blame on others, you are probably acting out an old family behavior. Even if blaming wasn't one of your family's most obvious strategies, it is a red flag because it always indicates that you're in a defensive posture—and you are most likely to reach for old coping mechanisms when you feel defensive.

Occasionally, the blame may seem justified. You may run into a person who seems impossibly difficult and uncommunicative, and you may have to ignore or work around that person. More often, however, you'll meet competent, well-meaning people who carry family baggage just as you do, and who sometimes get into difficult relationships with one another.

You'll know you're blaming others when you find yourself mulling over such thoughts as:

- This whole situation is Janice's fault.

- If Terry hadn't said that, everything would be fine.

- My life would be a lot easier if Vince didn't work here.

If you find yourself blaming or obsessing about another person, stop for a moment and ask yourself if that person, or his or her behavior, reminds you of anyone in your family. Do the feelings you are having remind you of feelings you had as a child? Use this red flag of blaming to pinpoint when, and around whom, you feel defensive. You may see a pattern, and can use that information to do the exercises in Part 3.

▣ RED FLAG #3: YOU FEEL ANXIOUS, AFRAID, ANGRY OR CONFUSED

Anxiety, fear, anger, and confusion are the most difficult emotions we face. These four feelings can often be painful, and most families' emotional survival strategies are specifically designed to mask, minimize, or suppress them. Of all the emotions, these four are the most likely to make you act as you did when you were a child and your family was in emotional turmoil.

Whenever you feel anxious, angry, afraid, or confused, be on the alert for the specific roles, rules, and ways of relating that you bring to work from your family. You'll discover what they are in Chapters 4–9. If you want to respond in a more positive way, you'll have to change that behavior consciously, using the exercises in Part 3.

When these feelings dominate your workplace, remember that *everyone* is more likely to fall back into their families' old behaviors and tactics.

▣ RED FLAG #4: YOU OFTEN FEEL DRAWN INTO CONFLICTS THAT AREN'T YOURS

Bill shifted in his seat as he watched his coworkers, Jeff and Dawn, vie for the most interesting parts of a team project. As the tension built between them, he became increasingly agitated and finally jumped in as a self-appointed mediator. Jeff and Dawn both turned on him—just as his boss and another coworker had done the week before when he'd tried to make peace between them, and just as his parents had always done when he tried to patch up their fights.

Children are often used as peacemakers in conflicts between their parents, between parents and other siblings, or between two siblings. They learn early on to assume responsibility for situations for which they should not be liable. This habit often follows them into adulthood and finds fertile ground at work, where there are always problems and conflicts to be resolved.

If you notice that you are worrying about other people's problems, trying to fix situations so that everyone is happy, or attempting to make peace between two people who are in conflict, think back to your childhood and ask yourself if you played that role in your family. If you did, see who was involved and why you wanted to fix the trouble between them. Did you want to be perceived as the Hero? Did you want peace at any cost and decide it would only happen if you made it happen?

I've seen in my practice that when my clients take on other people's problems, they almost inevitably wind up defending *themselves* with old family patterns. They've assumed responsibility for a situation over which they have no control. Sooner or later, they feel frustrated, hurt, or defensive and slide into their families' tactics for coping with these feelings.

▣ RED FLAG #5: YOU FEEL RESTRICTED, LIMITED, AND ONE-DIMENSIONAL

Have you ever felt as if the walls were closing in on you? Or that if you behaved differently from the way you behaved yesterday, people would notice and be upset with you? Or that you could only talk and act in certain limited ways?

In my practice, I've seen that when people feel restricted, boxed in, or stifled in these ways, they have usually gotten stuck in one of their families' old roles, rules, or ways of relating.

This red flag feels like tunnel vision. It may seem as if there is only one solution to a problem and you can't try anything else, even though that one solution isn't working. You may not deal well with new information or with change, and feel as if you have to monitor how you express yourself. You may feel compelled to play the office nice guy and never let yourself get angry or upset, or to be the one who always has an answer, so that you're never allowed a moment of hesitation or confusion. Your self-esteem may start to suffer, and so may your bottom line. You may feel as if you have to fight dirty just to break even. It may seem impossible to avoid competition with a coworker, just as it was impossible to escape sibling rivalry in your family.

When you feel stuck in only one particular mode of behavior, when you notice that you aren't being as productive or creative as usual, when you can't seem to find solutions, or when your options seem to be shrinking, examine the situation to see if any of the people or events involved remind you of home.

Try to remember a time in your childhood when you had that same frustrated feeling or felt as if you were hitting your head against a brick wall. What was the situation? What were you feeling? Who was involved? How had you been taught to react? Are you repeating that same reaction today?

▣ RED FLAG #6: YOU SEE RIPPLES IN YOUR OFFICE'S EMOTIONAL POND

When one person starts relating to others in the ways that he or she did as a child, it usually starts a chain reaction. When you engage in old family behaviors, the people around you are likely to engage in theirs—and vice versa. My clients are often amazed at how quickly one person's mood and behavior can ripple through the entire office.

◘ Production fell behind at Treats, Inc., and the operations director, Carl, used the same intimidation tactics he'd learned from his father to pressure the production manager, Dorothy, into bringing more muffins and cookies off the line. She felt persecuted and fell into her old family role of Victim. She formed an alliance with the chief financial officer, Grant, who listened to her complaints and slipped into his old role of Rescuer by telling the company president, Celeste, that Carl was overstepping both his bounds and his budget.

Carl's intimidation was like a stone thrown into a quiet pond. It rippled out and then back in again, triggering reactions in other people, who triggered reactions in others, until Treats, Inc. was tied up in knots and became completely unproductive.

When everyone around you seems to be acting in ways that are manipulative, defensive, or controlling, the ripple has probably begun. Be especially wary when your boss starts using defensive or repetitive strategies. Bosses' ripples tend to be bigger and to move more quickly than other people's ripples, because people often care more what bosses think of them and so are more likely to be triggered. Stress, like water, tends to flow down and out within an organization—and family patterns follow the stress wherever it goes. It usually begins with one boss, who passes it on to his or her staff, who pass it on to the people under them.

This process goes on and on—one person's old family strategies triggering another's, triggering another's, and so on—until somebody stops it. Someone else may have thrown the first stone, but the only way to stop the ripples is for you not to throw your stone. Step back and use the techniques in Chapter 10 to avoid contributing to the chaos by falling into one of your own defensive patterns.

◘ RED FLAG #7: YOU OR YOUR
    ORGANIZATION EXPERIENCE CHANGE

In family systems therapy, change of any kind is a red flag because the system is disrupted. People and their relationships with one another are thrown off balance. That makes everyone feel threatened, and defensive patterns are almost sure to emerge.

Change is also a hidden source of stress, the primary trigger for family-related patterns. We don't always recognize good changes as stressful, but your nerves may feel just as strained by getting promoted or landing the job of your dreams as by meeting bone-crushing deadlines with no staff to help you.

Change can be internal or external, major or minor, positive or negative, personal or professional. It can involve such events as marriage, death, birth, divorce, a new job, transfer to a new department, promotions or raises (yours or other people's), a new boss, new staff members, a new direction for the company, a downturn in business, people being fired—anything that represents a shift in your own situation, in your relationship with the organization, in how you relate to others, or in how they relate to you.

◘   The executive staff at Saint Francis Hospital had enjoyed generally productive, amicable relationships until Russ was chosen from among all the assistant directors to succeed the retiring executive director. Prior to his appointment, Russ had been just one of the executive gang who wasn't above a long lunch with a pitcher of margaritas at La Tortola. Since his promotion, however, he had become the most serious man alive, meticulous about propriety and a stickler for the rules—and he wasn't thrilled to see the people who were supposed to be running "his" institution guzzling margaritas at lunchtime. The stress of his new responsibilities triggered the role he had played in his family, that of Perfect Child.

This role severely restricted his ability to connect with his executive staff and was understandably stressful for the assistant directors as well. They perceived him as a Tyrant and, of course, defended themselves with *their* old family roles, rules, and ways of relating. Charlotte, the personnel director, became the office Clown and threw herself into inappropriate activities like throwing Russ a birthday party featuring an exotic dancer jumping out of a cake. Neal, the community relations director, fell back into the Rebel role he had played in his family in reaction to Russ's new demands for hard work and propriety. Everyone's behavior became extremely rigid and restricted by the roles they used to defend themselves against the discomfort of change, and business at Saint Francis nearly ground to a halt.

Change is a test of organizations as well as individuals. Each must maintain a delicate balance between being stable and being flexible. Both the visible and the invisible roles, rules, and ways of relating have to be strong enough to give people a clear sense of who they are and what is expected of them, but flexible enough to accommodate change and growth.

During stressful changes like the one at Saint Francis, both individuals and organizations tend to tighten up and become somewhat rigid in order to deal with chaos and confusion. An organization that frowns on people taking sick days to deal with personal matters might become even stricter in this area. A manager might turn what she once called a "guideline" for her staff into an unwritten rule requiring that they answer memos from other departments within twenty-four hours.

Periods of peak stress for companies might include annual report time, board meetings, stockholders' meetings, new management, takeovers, new hiring policies, new offices, staff cutbacks, new markets, impaired markets, or new competition within a market. (For individuals, the stress might peak both at these times and also in tandem with performance evaluations, the introduction of new department members or new bosses, or staff cutbacks.)

Tightening up roles, rules, and ways of relating temporarily during these times can be effective if they loosen up again when the crisis has passed. If the rigidity gets too severe or if it becomes chronic, however, either the organization or its people may be so impaired that they can no longer function effectively.

In organizations, this rigidity often takes the form of protecting the status quo. Problems are ignored, hidden, or denied. No one talks about the fact that the company isn't doing well or that people are unhappy working there. Differences among people are suppressed, and tension builds up. There is no way to relieve the stress, people feel defensive and threatened, and everybody starts reaching for old family behaviors to protect themselves. The more inflexible the organization becomes, the more quickly and strongly those family patterns take hold, and the more they dominate the company.

(Organizations can also create stress and invite old family behaviors by being *too* open and flexible. Some people get uneasy when the rules aren't clear enough or the organization doesn't provide enough structure, certainty, and stability. Several of my clients have felt extremely unsettled and tense working for laid-back, hang-loose companies with very few visible rules or structures.)

If the ways that people relate to one another and do business within your organization can adjust to change while still providing a baseline of security for people, then you will see fewer unhealthy behaviors. People can relax and relate to one another more openly and honestly. They can discuss the changes and their feelings about them, air and resolve problems, and find innovative solutions. They can be themselves, talk about what they think and feel, and work through their difficulties. Stress can be released and people don't need to resort to destructive family patterns in order to protect themselves. They can concentrate on doing their jobs.

The balancing act between stability and flexibility is difficult because there are no hard and fast rules for how rigid, or how flexible, a corporation undergoing change should be. For a time, you have to work without a safety net, play it by ear, and learn to balance yourself without handrails before the equilibrium is restored.

The following symptoms are found in all organizations, but they are stronger and more pervasive in companies that are so rigid that they cannot handle stress well. Whether the situation is temporary or chronic, you will know that your changing organization is likely to foster ineffective family patterns when:

- *Management is on the defensive.* When there are problems, the unhealthy organization's leadership cloisters itself away and comes up with a list of people or conditions to blame: the economy, union demands, politicians, unfair competition, etc. No one takes responsibility for problems or for finding solutions.

- *The organization doesn't bounce back from internal or external changes.* If the president passes away, for instance, the company can't replace him. If the markets change, the company doesn't expand its vision to deal with the problem and investigate new markets.

- *Management gives mixed messages and doesn't take a clear stand on issues.* They say they want people to communicate openly and work through differences but provide no structures in which this can be done—and those who try it are seen as oddballs or troublemakers. The rules change from person to person, from month to month, and from situation to situation—and people stop trusting what management says.

- *The company is managed by crisis and is always in a state of emergency.* Everybody's energy goes into putting out fires. Poor financial planning results in a desperate need for short-term gains, and everyone gets caught up in the drama. The president comes up with his idea of a brilliant marketing concept over dinner one night, and the organization is turned upside down to implement it the next morning. People have no idea when they'll be forced to drop everything and save the company from disaster.

- *Staff are not kept informed of changes or problems.* Employees are treated as children who can't handle the truth, and important information is withheld from them.

- *Management looks for quick fixes rather than long-term solutions.* The focus is on alleviating such symptoms as high absenteeism with threats and punishment rather than on dealing with causes—like disrespectful management practices. Seven middle managers quit because of an offensive policy, and the company scrambles to replace them rather than to examine the policy or how it was implemented.

- *You can't talk about feelings or conflicts with others.* Feelings are considered inappropriate and unprofessional. There is an unwritten law against rocking the boat. Working through difficulties with others is considered disruptive.

- *You can't talk about problems in the company or better ways of doing things, even if new systems could make you more productive.* Management just hopes that problems will go away or that no one will notice them. Higher-ups focus on plodding along, protecting their positions, and maintaining the status quo—not looking for innovative improvements.

• *You have to protect your boss and other managers by hiding their mistakes.* Even if your boss is incompetent, lazy, abusive, or impaired by personal problems or addictions, you have to make sure that he or she looks good. You do the extra work and put up with bad management and bad behavior, and your boss gets all the credit.

• *People feel defensive, as if they have to protect their places in the organization.* They don't feel secure in their jobs, appreciated for their contribution, or recognized as human beings with valuable ideas. They think the company is using them for its own gain, and that it treats them like cogs in a wheel. They don't trust that they'll be rewarded with promotions or raises if there is any way the company can avoid it. Coworkers, staff, and bosses are seen as antagonists and competitors who might take what belongs to them.

• *The organization is run by secrets, underground pacts, and clandestine alliances.* You play the game, or you don't get anywhere. If you don't jump into the snake pit, you abdicate your influence and power.

If you experience any of these conditions in your company, remember that you're at risk to react with your family's old habits and emotional dynamics. Notice that you are probably feeling defensive, and take note of which invisible roles, rules, and ways of relating are your automatic reactions. Use the techniques in Chapter 10 to ease the situation and the exercises in Part 3 to make changes that help you cope with change—in your own situation or your organization—in more effective and productive ways.

◩ BEFORE YOU GO ON . . .

In this chapter, I've laid out the conditions in which you are most likely to fall back into old family patterns. In the next several chapters, you'll look specifically at what some of those patterns are. As the exact roles, rules, and ways of relating that you bring to work from your family become clearer, you are likely to feel the very thing that those old strategies were designed to mask: discomfort.

That's good. It means you're getting close to seeing your own part in difficult relationships, and that is the first step in making productive changes. But as we've noted, discomfort often prompts us to blame others. We all have a tendency to look for the people wearing black hats, but it's also important to remember that respect for others is crucial in this work and that none of us can know for sure what another person is thinking or feeling. As you explore your own patterns in more depth, keep in mind that your office's emotional environment is an intricate system in which everybody plays a part, but for which no one individual is responsible.

In the next six chapters, I'll describe the strategies people use most frequently to defend against stressful situations at work. Make a mental note if you recognize one that you use. You'll use this information to do the exercises in Part 3.

4

Big Daddy: Dealing with "Oppressive" Authority

We have seen how easy it is to slip back into the roles we played as children when relationships at work become stressful. In this chapter, we will discuss three invisible roles—the Rebel, the Victim, and the Rescuer—to which people often revert in the face of authority figures who are oppressive, or whom they *perceive* as being oppressive. We'll also discuss the role of the Oppressor or Tyrant.

We're often unaware that we're playing these invisible roles. Pinpointing which we're most likely to adopt under stress is the first step in developing more authentic, productive, and nurturing relationships with people at work. Roles play an essential part in supporting an unhealthy emotional system's equilibrium.

As you read, see if you recognize yourself in any of these roles. Note what you learn about yourself; you'll be using this information to do the exercises in Part 3.

▣ "OPPRESSIVE" AUTHORITY

How people relate to authority—especially authority that they perceive as demanding, oppressive, ruthless, judgmental, overbearing,
opinionated, uncaring, or cruel—is almost always determined by their
experience with authority in their families. If one or both of your parents were angry, compulsive, abusive, judgmental, or highly critical—
and used fear to maintain discipline and get their messages
across—then you may have developed a habit of defending yourself
against these behaviors early in life, and you may be at risk for one of
the roles or strategies described in this chapter.

The Oppressor may be your boss, a colleague, or even someone who
works for you. It's the person around about whom you feel defensive,
persecuted, or in danger of losing respect.

Some bosses are truly overbearing and tyrannical, but often oppression is in the eye of the beholder. Two people who grew up in different families may see the world, and its bosses and authority figures,
in entirely different ways. Some Oppressors are created by the oppressed.

People who already have a tendency to gravitate toward the roles
of Rebel, Victim, or Rescuer often perceive an authority figure as
oppressive even when the person in charge isn't behaving that way,
just so they can justify acting out the roles in which they feel comfortable—and at which they are experts. If Jenny grew up as the Victim in her family, she is more likely to perceive her boss as an
Oppressor than someone who is more comfortable in another role that
does not require the presence of an Oppressor. Allen, for instance,
might be more comfortable in the Superachiever role and perceive
the same boss to be weak or ineffectual so that he can rush in and save
the day.

We all have our own individual, family-bred reactions to authority.
The three people described in this chapter all resorted to different roles
to protect themselves against their discomfort, and your reaction may
be entirely different from theirs. The important thing is to recognize
what your own specific defenses are so that you can choose whether you
want to continue using them.

▣ REBEL WITH A SHAKY CAUSE

Burke was a born salesman—and a classic Rebel who fought back against authority. He told me he had trouble keeping jobs because his bosses had all been "cutthroat" or "unreasonable" and Burke always felt he was fending off their "attacks."

Burke was on the road most of the time for TravelComp, which sold software to the travel industry, and his new boss Dennis phoned him three times every day demanding detailed reports on how much business Burke had done by eleven o'clock, by two o'clock, and by the end of the day. If the results weren't extraordinary, he would bark, "Hey, what's wrong!?" Burke's instinctive reaction was to put up his fists and come out fighting. After a few weeks he exploded at Dennis, "Get off my back! I can't do my job if you treat me like I'm nine years old."

Burke's belligerent reaction made the situation even worse. Dennis became even more rigid and demanding, their conversations were barely civil, and Burke wasted so much time trying to win his fights with Dennis that he didn't meet his sales goals and quit TravelComp three months later.

Burke's reaction seems natural and justifiable given the overbearing and controlling nature of Dennis's frequent calls and sharp accusations. Yet Burke was falling back into one of his family roles in dealing with Dennis, one that only caused him more stress and frustration. Although he could not change Dennis's behavior, he could change his experience of it.

Burke told me, "When these guys start getting in my face, they seem to be saying I don't know what I'm doing, and I do!" He felt frustrated and out of control—exactly the way he had always felt around his father. As we talked, he began to see where his pattern of reactive rebellion had begun.

Burke's father was a successful attorney who ruled the household with an iron hand and made a point of checking Burke's homework every night. Burke squirmed under this scrutiny, and when he got to high school he decided to show his father who was boss. He started drinking, hung out with a crowd that was always in trouble, and barely graduated.

Burke's rebellion made his father's life miserable, and that gave Burke a certain power over the older man at a time when he felt desperately out of control. Since then, rebelling and acting out had been his automatic response to anyone he thought was scrutinizing and judging him.

When Burke saw that his instinct to rebel was just a habit, a knee-jerk reaction to events twenty years in the past, he realized that he had some choices. He didn't have to react as he had when he was fifteen or remain a prisoner of his relationship with his father. He began to take charge (using techniques we'll explore in Chapter 10, especially No-Fault Thinking and avoiding the Doom Loop). He also started making specific changes to avoid the Rebel role, using the exercises in Part 3.

The transformation didn't happen overnight. On his next job, Burke often caught himself slipping into rebellious reactions, but recognizing them for what they were—old habits that were no longer useful to him—allowed him to stop and choose whether he wanted to continue behaving that way. The process reminded him of the month after he'd quit smoking and caught himself reaching into his pocket for a cigarette, only to find nothing there, remember a positive choice he'd made, and reach into his other pocket for a stick of gum instead. That had felt awkward at first, too—but Burke applied the same persistence to developing a new relationship with authority that he had to stopping smoking.

At first, Burke could hardly believe it was that simple, that so much trouble had resulted just from relating to bosses as he'd related to his father. As he explored that relationship further, many complexities emerged—but the basic understanding of why he always rebelled proved to be his most powerful tool in breaking a painful and destructive pattern of behavior. This knowledge became the cornerstone of more productive and pleasant relationships with his bosses, and the beginning of a happier and more successful career.

The Rebel Role

People who play the Rebel role are also known as black sheep or troublemakers. Rebels may cause trouble at school, get bad grades, run around with a crowd their parents don't like, and do whatever they can to disrupt their parents'—and society's—status quo. As adults, Rebels may lead uprisings at work, quit their jobs, or become so abrasive that they get fired.

You may be acting out the Rebel role if you find yourself constantly at odds with the system, going toe-to-toe with bosses, stirring up coworkers against management, or giving vent to your anger in inappropriate ways.

▣ THE VEHEMENT VICTIM

Ruth's Victim role reached crisis proportions when she worked as a purchasing agent for a large manufacturing company.

Her boss Sam was always hovering over her, literally looking over her shoulder to be sure she didn't make mistakes. Communication was an oppressive one-way street: He talked, she listened. Ruth didn't feel respected or trusted, but instead of speaking directly to Sam about her experience, she became quiet and withdrawn. She started confiding in Abby, who worked in Accounting, and told her every terrible, judgmental, uncaring thing that Sam did. "He thinks he owns me," Ruth said to Abby. "He always wants me to work overtime and demands perfection. I'm sick of it. This company isn't going to get another ounce of energy out of me."

Abby was sympathetic and comforting. She shook her head and wondered how Ruth made it through the day. They agreed to have coffee every morning so Ruth could "outflow."

Talking to Abby made Ruth feel a little better for about fifteen minutes every morning. It released just enough of the pressure that Ruth never felt compelled to talk directly to Sam—but she felt worse and worse about herself and how she was doing her job. Abby's emotional bandages actually kept Ruth from dealing with the problem and finding a solution.

Ruth came to me because Sam gave her a poor performance evaluation. We discovered, among other things, that her mother had been a lot like Sam. Ruth called her "a demanding physician" who had insisted on having everything her own way. She wanted Ruth and her brother to be model children—honor students, perfectly behaved, popular—and made them feel as if they were being disloyal to the family if they failed to excel.

Ruth felt like a victim of this imposing woman's drive toward perfection. Instead of standing up to her mother, Ruth withdrew into resentment and formed an alliance with her sympathetic father that "rescued" her from her intrusive and overbearing mother. Now, whenever she was uncomfortable with someone in authority, she did the same thing. She withdrew emotionally, became a Victim, and looked around for someone to comfort her.

Recognizing this pattern gave Ruth power. If her own behavior was the source of the problem, then she could do something about it. She began using some of the empowering techniques in Chapter 10, especially the guidelines for disengaging from unhealthy emotional triangles. She stopped using Abby as a listening post and began talking directly to Sam. She told him that she didn't feel trusted when he looked over her shoulder and set up a regular time each week to meet with him about her job. When Sam saw that she actually did get more done when he wasn't hovering, he gained a new respect for her, and they developed into a highly productive, mutually supportive team.

The Victim Role

People who learned to play the Victim in childhood often fear conflict and feel insecure, invaded, criticized, out of control, or incompetent around people whom they perceive as oppressive or judgmental. They may doubt themselves and think they aren't doing enough. Often, they put the job first and their own needs second, until finally they either lose themselves entirely or become so resentful that they begin "accidentally on purpose" making mistakes that make the boss look bad. If they find a confidant who agrees with them about their sorry state and "rescues" them from the stress, they can stay stuck almost indefinitely.

At one time or another, most of us have indulged in the Victim's self-pity, preferring complaining to dealing directly with a person or situation—especially if we felt persecuted by an institution or person we perceived as more powerful than ourselves: a boss, a board of directors, a coworker, a customer, the IRS, a competitor, market changes, etc. Problems arise when we play this part *repeatedly* and *automatically,* without even being aware of what we are doing.

▣ REVELING IN THE RESCUE

Ted played the role of informal Counselor or Rescuer at a small, up-and-coming clothing manufacturer whose president, Jerry, was a hard-driving and somewhat abrasive workaholic. The second time Ted was passed over for a promotion, he asked Jerry what was wrong and was told, "You should take some of your own advice." When Ted asked him what he meant, Jerry said, "You're always giving people advice about how to deal with me, and it feels as if you're going behind my back—so I don't trust you. Let me handle my own staff."

When Ted came to see me, he said, "But I like helping them. It makes me feel good." He'd been taking care of other people for as long as he could remember. His father had been a stern, unemotional minister, and Ted had distinguished himself from the other five children in his rather cold, undemonstrative family by being "the one who had feelings." His brothers and sisters all came to him for advice and comfort when they were in trouble with their father. He had won attention and acknowledgment by being the kind and caring Rescuer, and his father had never bothered him too much because Ted was so popular with the others.

As an adult, Ted was still trying to circumvent oppressive authority by being the caring Counselor who earned love and attention by helping others deal with their problems, and was off-limits to the dangerous person in charge. He started to turn this habit around by using the techniques for taking charge in Chapter 10, especially by becoming an objective observer and disengaging from emotional triangles, and began taking the six steps in Part 3 to be free of his Rescuer role.

The Rescuer Role

Wherever there are Victims, there are Rescuers. Rescuers' response to "oppressive" authority is to rush to comfort or take care of the "oppressed." They are the third ingredient of what we call in family systems therapy the Persecutor-Victim-Rescuer emotional triangle. This is one of the most common phenomena in both workplaces and families.

In families, Rescuers are the children who anticipate problems among family members and head them off. Their job is to save one family member from another's oppressive, critical, or judgmental behavior. You may have played the role of Rescuer if you came to the aid of a sibling who was always being teased or beaten up by another sibling, if you protected one of your parents from the other, or if you protected a sibling from a parent.

In the workplace, Rescuers are usually seen as good-hearted, selfless souls. They feel valued and needed when they are helping or saving someone—but focusing on others acts as a distraction from their own uncomfortable situations, which then never get resolved. Riding in on a white horse also creates dependency in the Victims they are trying to help.

If you find yourself drawn to Victims, worrying about a coworker's problems with an oppressive boss or an unreasonable colleague, feeling responsible for the emotional well-being of everyone in the department, or being constantly called upon to give advice on work issues and relationships, then you may be slipping into the role of Rescuer. You may become so identified with this role that you function as the Caretaker for everyone. Caretakers are like Rescuers, with the added twist that the Caretaker doesn't need a Victim to rescue. To a Caretaker, everyone needs help.

◘   IF YOU ARE THE PERSECUTOR. . .

Every Victim needs a Persecutor. It's not surprising that managers, supervisors, or people in authority often take on this role just because of their position in the hierarchy. But this isn't always the case. Individual employees can and do persecute each other with power games, verbal assaults, backstabbing, and needling. In addition, some of my clients who do not have line-management responsibility have found themselves treated as if they are in the role of Persecutor or Tyrant by people acting as Rebels, Victims, or Rescuers. For example, if you say no to someone, take an unpopular stand with coworkers, or refuse to involve yourself in emotional triangles, your healthy behavior may land you the label of Persecutor without you earning it. Also, it's possible that under pressure you may occasionally resort to behaviors that are typical of the Persecutor role. If you experience yourself being placed in this role by others, notice how this happens and in what circumstances. If you are merely being labeled unfairly, do not change your behavior. Your thoughtful and adult actions will eventually reap positive results. Make sure, though, that the accusations *are* misdirected. Could you be a true Persecutor? Think about your childhood experiences. What role was most familiar?

A true Persecutor behaves in angry or retaliatory ways to make things happen or uses fear to motivate. Some of the behaviors associated with the Persecutor/Tyrant role include the use of threats, humiliation, harsh demands, put-downs, and rigid enforcement of rules to force compliance. This role is often based on a belief that most people are basically incompetent, lazy, or dishonest and need to be pushed and forced to do the right thing.

If you tend to adopt the Persecutor role in your work relationships to get a job done, take a look at what you gain from this and how it may mirror a dynamic from your family. Think about what kind of people and circumstances prompt you to play this role today. It may seem like the only way to get things done, but the cost is usually high. At the very least, it's an ineffective way to make friends and provides only a temporary way to influence people. At worse, it can damage your and others' self-esteem and destroy relationships.

Although the Persecutor may be a difficult one with which to identify personally, remember that you can use the tools described in Chapter 10 and the six steps in Part 3 to break the pattern.

◙ BIG DADDY AND BIG BROTHER

Be on the lookout for a subtle phenomenon that has crept into the American corporate environment. In many ways, the corporation itself has come to be considered a controlling, uncaring Persecutor whose oppressive policies ride roughshod over people's lives. It's easy to react to your corporation as you might to an oppressive boss and to slip into one of the roles described in this chapter.

You might, for instance, become a Victim of the aggressive corporate giant . . . or a Rebel who takes on Goliath against all odds and loses . . . or a Rescuer attempting to save coworkers from the ruthless Tyrant. . . . Or you may jump into whatever role you used to deal with oppression as a child.

Genuine corporate offenses need to be addressed, but plunging headlong into one of these family-patterned roles in reaction to your company as a whole is almost never an effective strategy.

▣ QUESTIONS TO ASK YOURSELF

You may be playing the Persecutor, the Rebel, the Victim, or the Rescuer in your office—or you may have another reaction to authority that isn't covered in this chapter. Being aware of what role you're likely to adopt is your most powerful tool in avoiding these behaviors and their unproductive consequences.

Answer these questions to start exploring how you relate to "oppressive" authority:

- Who is the "Oppressor" who stirs things up in your office?

- How do you feel and act around this person? Angry? Afraid? Protective? What other reactions do you have?

- What is it about the person in authority that gets to you? What does he or she do, say, or communicate nonverbally that feels threatening?

- Recall the last time you had a problem with this person. What was your first, instinctive reaction? Did you want to smack him or her? Run away? Tell your troubles to someone? Save the person h or she was abusing? What other response did you have?

- Can you identify the role you played? Rebel? Victim? Rescuer? Another role?

- How did you react to the person who was the authority in your family when you were a child? Do you often react in similar ways to authority today?

It's not always easy to see your own part in these scenarios. If you're having trouble, the exercises in Part 3 will help you pinpoint the exact emotional dynamics operating in your situation and what you can do to change what's not working for you.

5

Martyr Mamas: Manipulating with Guilt

Martyrs in an office may give up their weekends, let coworkers have the best lunch hour, or bend over backward for their staffs, but they'll return later for people's first-born children, life's savings—or jobs. They're doing everything for the people around them—and they want those people to know it. Their real message is: *Somebody owes me—big time!*

In family systems therapy, we've seen that people often adopt the Martyr role as a reaction to the stress of feeling out of control in their relationships with others. *Martyrs learned in their families to use guilt, confusion, and shame to control others' behavior and get others to do what they want.*

They may only want respect, attention, or affection, but one way or another, they demand from other people a payback to which those people never agreed. They are similar to Victims, except that they never suffer in silence. They want the world to know just how much they're doing or giving up for the sake of another person or the company, and they want a payback.

The invisible role of Martyr may show up in workplaces more than any other family-based pattern for two reasons:

1. *Martyrdom is a quiet, well-behaved role* that doesn't look as messy or seem to cause as many problems as, for instance, the troublemaking Rebel role or the nasty Persecutor role. Martyrs appear to be the good guys who were just standing there when the train came by and ran them over. They are subtle and covert—they don't usually break rules or get into obvious conflict with authority—so they can hide out in a company more easily than people who play flashier roles.

2. *Many of us had at least one parent who played the role of Martyr.* The traditional and sometimes suffocating roles demanded of women during the forties, fifties, and sixties frequently gave rise to martyrlike behavior. Although this is changing today, the role of Martyr is still part of the repertoire of emotional roles that overworked parents of both sexes often adopt. We may learn early in life how to use martyrdom and see the control it gives the Martyr over other people—however temporary, destructive, or superficial that control might be.

If you learned the Martyr role in your family, you may feel that people take advantage of your generosity, or that others don't pull their weight, or that you don't get enough recognition for all the extra work you do.

It can be uncomfortable to see the Martyr in ourselves, but most of us have acted out this invisible role at some point—with people above us, below us, or parallel to us in the organization. Understanding what triggers this pattern can be tremendously empowering. You can then take the steps outlined in Part 3 to change your behavior and reclaim power in relationships at work. As you read, think about when, and around whom, you are most likely to fall into the Martyr role.

▣ THREE MARTYR "LOOKS"

Martyrs wear many disguises and can appear at any level in a company:

* *"Nice" bosses* who are generous and caring—until there's a crisis
* *Saintly coworkers* who give their colleagues the better vacation times or do more than their share but demand an enormous payback when the other people least expect it

- *Martyred employees* who don't mind working until nine o'clock every night but have an unwritten, unstated expectation that it's going to win them a raise, a promotion, or at least a lot of strokes—and who are outraged when others don't go along with their hidden agendas.

Being a Martyr buys you some small measure of temporary control over the people around you—but because the Martyr role is highly manipulative, you sacrifice self-esteem and honest, supportive relationships. This role also demands that you act as if you don't have any power, so that people will feel shamed or guilt-tripped into feeling sorry for you and doing what you want—but the more you act as if you don't have any power, the less power you actually have.

Martyrs yearn for sympathy, attention, and admiration—but often they generate more resentment, anger, and withdrawal. Typical reactions to the Martyr role involve feelings of resentment, frustration, and guilt covered up by a combination of behaviors such as capitulation and silent withdrawal or angry outbursts. People who play the Martyr role will often play the Victim when confronted about their behavior. People usually wind up either capitulating to the Martyr's guilt trip or standing up for themselves and looking like the bad guy. Neither course of action is much fun or generates much self-esteem.

See if you recognize yourself in any of these Martyr disguises.

The "Nice" Boss

Kevin managed a sporting goods store and gave his employees every perk and benefit he possibly could: outrageous discounts on store merchandise, passes to local ball games, and generous overtime. In return, he expected them to bend over backward for him—only he never told them that.

When the economy dipped and people stopped spending as much money on tennis rackets, warm-up suits, and workout equipment, Kevin called in his markers. He pressed the staff for longer hours, extra work, and high-pressure sales tactics. He talked about teamwork (translate: "I've been on your team; now it's your turn to be on mine") and even said, "Look, I've done a lot for you guys. You owe me."

Two staff members balked at the new regime and quit. One told Kevin, "I never agreed to work six days a week, ten hours a day. I don't care how much overtime you pay, that wasn't part of our deal." A third did as she was asked but became withdrawn, resentful, and unproductive.

Kevin was hurt and angry. How could these people betray him when he'd done so much for them? As we talked, he saw that he'd made many assumptions that he hadn't shared with his staff—in part because he'd been afraid they wouldn't stick by him if the going got tough—and that he had become a Martyr to control their behavior and ensure their loyalty with guilt. Ironically, his behavior produced just the opposite result. People resented his attempt to control them and either walked out or became unproductive.

Kevin had learned the invisible role of Martyr from his father, who "sacrificed his health and well-being," working sixty hours a week to provide a nice home, good schools, and lavish presents for his wife and children. The father's hidden agenda was that everything had to be done his way. He insisted on his wife staying at home, and all the kids eventually chose professions that reflected what the father wanted them to be when they grew up.

Now Kevin was learning what the Martyr role could cost him: self-esteem, a productive staff, and possibly his store. The good news was that, having recognized that he tended to fall into the Martyr role, Kevin could change his behavior. He could relate to his staff in a more straightforward way, tell them what he wanted and expected, ask directly whether or not they were willing to give it, and negotiate arrangements on which everyone agreed.

The Coworker "from Heaven"

Angie was one of five assistant administrators for a large Detroit charity. She worked extravagant hours and was always glad to help the other assistant administrators with their work, saying, "Well, if one of us falls behind, we all suffer. I don't mind working a little harder to avoid that."

This martyred attitude didn't endear her to her colleagues, who were slow to defend Angie when her budget was slashed during a financial shakeup. She eventually shamed all of them into supporting her, since, as she reminded them, they would have been in trouble as well if she hadn't helped them with their work. Grudgingly, each assistant administrator went to bat for her.

Their support carried weight and Angie got her budget—but her colleagues agreed not to accept her help in the future because it gave her too much leverage. They didn't like being manipulated, and Angie found herself out in the cold. The situation was so uncomfortable that she quit six months later.

Angie had learned the Martyr role from her mother, who used guilt to control her children, constantly reminding them that she was a single mother who worked all day and all night for them and that they should not only do their chores but stay home Saturday night and keep her company.

Angie had learned to turn the tables on her mother, racing home from school to perform some Herculean task—waxing the floors, polishing the silver, or doing the laundry—before asking her mother if she could go on a weekend trip with her friends or buy a new outfit.

Without being aware of it, Angie reached for the Martyr role whenever she felt control slipping through her hands. Manipulating people with guilt and shame had become her automatic reaction to feeling powerless, and she had to work hard to break the habit.

The Martyred Staff

Ellen worked as a secretary for three math professors at a community college and felt frustrated and out of control because these three women didn't coordinate her work with one another, so none of them knew what the others had given her to do. Ellen always felt pressured, behind, out of control, and as if she were doing three times the work and getting a third of the acknowledgment.

She wanted her bosses to know that she was overworked and underrecognized, and that she wanted some attention and sympathy—but she didn't know how to tell them. Instead, she reacted to the stress with her old, family-patterned Martyr role. She let mountains of file folders stack up on her desk, dissolved into silent tears periodically throughout the day, and developed a habit of burying her head in her hands, then rushing out of the office and hiding out in the restroom for a half hour. If anyone asked what was wrong, Ellen just shook her head, waved a damp tissue, and stammered, "Oh, I'll be okay. Just let me get back to work."

She fell more and more behind, and eventually her worst fear came true. She was fired, and that brought her to me.

In Ellen's family, everybody had tried to outmartyr one another. Her mother had divorced Ellen's father when Ellen was two and her sister was four. The mother played the abandoned woman and Martyr to get the girls to behave ("After all your father did to me, now you're crying and want to stay up late"), but her daughters were quick studies and the Martyr role boomeranged on her. Ellen and her sister knew their mother felt guilty about the divorce, and that they only needed to squeeze out a few tears and appear "damaged" to get anything they wanted from her.

The position at the community college was only Ellen's second job, and she was just beginning to learn that the rest of the world wasn't quite as vulnerable to martyrdom as her mother had been—and to see that she would have to break that habit in order to succeed.

▣   WHERE THE MARTYR IS BORN

Many of us learned as children that we could get what we wanted by making others, usually our parents but also our siblings, feel guilty and confused.

- "That's okay, Mom. I'll clean the house on Saturday. My bike is too old to keep up with the other kids anyway." ("That's okay, Evelyn. I've been putting in so many hours I don't have much of a social life anyway.")

- "I was hoping you'd be proud of me for getting great grades. I didn't know I had to be home on time, *too*." ("So I guess the great work I did on the Smith account doesn't count now, and I can't make one tiny mistake on this new project.")

We got the short-term results and thought, consciously or unconsciously, *this works!* We didn't realize we were developing a habit and that, for adults in the workplace, martyrdom would not be worth the cost in terms of self-esteem, respectful relationships, and even careers.

The people most at risk to play the Martyr role are those whose siblings or parents were always reminding them, "Look at all I'm doing and sacrificing for you. You're really going to owe me someday." The words don't have to be spoken; Martyrs can deliver this message loud and clear without ever saying a word.

It's natural for parents to make sacrifices for their children, but martyred parents are those who use these sacrifices to manipulate their kids. They make the children feel guilty because they gave up time, money, fun, a marriage, a fulfilling personal or professional life, friendships, leisure activities, going back to school or work, sex, or whatever—and now the children have to pay them back by doing what the parent wants or fulfilling some emotional need that the parent isn't getting fulfilled elsewhere.

For instance, a martyred father might feel such a lack of sympathy and affection from his wife that he complains to his children so that they will fulfill these needs. He might guilt-trip his children into everything from taking him to the movies, to mowing the lawn, to supporting him in his old age.

◙ QUESTIONS TO ASK YOURSELF

Few people respect Martyrs, and few people choose to be around them. It's not a pleasant or productive pattern—but it is just that, a pattern or habit over which you can take control. Whether or not your parents were Martyrs, ask yourself the following questions to see if you may be playing the Martyr role:

• Who treats you unfairly and puts unreasonable demands on you—your boss, your coworkers, or your staff?

• Do the people around you often seem guilty or confused?

• Do you ever find yourself keeping secret books on what others owe you and showing up unexpectedly to be repaid?

- Can you remember a time when you got what you wanted by playing the Martyr in your family?

- Do you think you have to manipulate people into giving you any one of these three things: (1) *paybacks,* such as promotions, returned favors, raises, vacations, etc.? (2) *attention, appreciation, affection,* or *sympathy?* (3) *emotional power* that comes when others are guilty or fearful around you?

6

Sibling Rivalry: Competing for a Place

Have you ever watched coworkers scurry around, competing for the boss's attention and approval? Have you ever seen yourself jump into the fray, feeling as if you were six years old and hating what you were doing—but apparently unable to stop yourself?

We've all done that at some point. It's only natural to want attention from people who are important to us. The problem arises when we try to get that attention at other people's expense, when we do it unconsciously, or when we use a six-year-old's tools and tactics in a business setting.

▣ CARVING OUT YOUR NICHE

Most of us learned as children that the best way to compete for recognition was to carve out a unique, special place for ourselves in the family—to establish a distinct, separate identity that made us different from everybody else. If one place or identity was taken—"best behaved," "artistic," "worst behaved"—we simply found another.

Under the stress of competition at work, which can be clandestine but ruthless, this is the strategy that most of us use—and we usually fall back on the exact roles that we used in our families. Often, people's special identity comes from one of the four invisible roles we'll cover in this chapter:

1. *The Superachiever* who excels in order to get noticed

2. *The "Bad" Child* who gets attention by taking the blame for everything and can't do anything right

3. *The Clown or Jokester* who tries to make people happy and be everybody's friend

4. *The Quiet "Good" Child* who actually gets attention by disappearing into the woodwork and not causing any more trouble in an already stressful situation.

As you read, notice if you tend to slip into any of these roles.

The Superachiever: "I Can Do Anything Better Than You"

When Elaine and Mark started working as loan agents for Federal Savings, a not-so-friendly competition developed between them almost immediately. Their boss Ben encouraged the rivalry because he thought they would both write more loans. He told them that people who didn't give this job 100 percent often fell through the cracks.

Elaine took the bait. She put in long hours, made cold calls, developed contacts in real estate offices, and generally devoted her life to producing results at Federal. At first, she seemed to thrive on the crisis and competition. She felt a rush of elation as her sales figures surged ahead of Mark's and Ben lavished her with praise.

After six months, however, Elaine realized that there would be no letting up. The more she produced, the more Ben wanted from her. She'd earned her place at Federal as a Superachiever; now she was stuck with the reputation and had to keep coming up with miracles. She was already operating at 100 percent and had nowhere to go, so she came to see me.

As we talked, Elaine saw that she had also played the role of Superachiever to get her mother's attention away from her younger brother, Doug. The only way Elaine could get noticed was to earn straight A's, lead her softball team to the city championship, spend every Saturday morning cleaning the house, and get elected to the student council.

She hadn't been aware that she was re-creating this same identity at Federal. Becoming a Superachiever had simply been her first, instinctive response to competition with her "brother" Mark and the "sibling rivalry" that Ben encouraged. When she understood that she'd been acting by rote, she started making changes, using the Six Action Steps in Part 3. She won both men's respect when she told them that she would continue to do her best, but that she wouldn't be driven crazy by unrealistic goals and expectations.

People who respond to competition by becoming Superachievers are often first children, who feel compelled to prove their worth and earn a place by doing more, and doing it better, than anyone else. This role can also be masked behind the disguise of the People Pleaser, who keeps everyone happy and maintains peace at any price.

The "Bad" Child: "I Can't Do Anything Right"

Superachievers try to do everything right; "Bad" Children use the opposite tactic to get attention and recognition. They do everything wrong and build their identities around being the family or office "Bad" Boy or "Bad" Girl.

Karen and Pete were both information coordinators at an insurance company. She didn't like or trust him because he was "always promoting himself and being the center of attention"—especially with their boss, Adele. He made a point of getting his work done early and asking Adele if there was anything else he could do to help. Karen fumed when Adele beamed and said she'd find an extra project for him since he was so competent and cooperative.

It seemed that the only time Adele noticed Karen was when Karen didn't finish her work or when she made mistakes. Then all the attention shifted from Pete to her. It was a stressful, negative kind of attention, but it was attention nevertheless. Karen started making more and more mistakes, not meeting deadlines, and soon became the person people blamed whenever anything was wrong. She was wise enough to figure out the elements in this equation—bad work equals attention—and came to me because she didn't want to get fired.

"In every job I've had, I've ended up feeling like a bad kid," she said. Karen's older sister was a lot like Pete—outgoing, popular, and a high achiever. Karen couldn't compete and tried to get recognition in the opposite way. She got low grades and always seemed to be in trouble. It was negative attention, but she established an identity and carved out a place for herself in the family. People knew just what to expect from her.

Now, so did Adele. Without being aware of what she was doing, Karen had tried to relieve the stress of competition with Pete by carving out the same place for herself at the insurance company that she had carved out in her family. Not surprisingly, the result was that she only created more stress—until she starting using the Six Action Steps in Part 3 to change her relationships with both Pete and Adele.

People who establish a place for themselves at work by being the scapegoat or "Bad" Child were often defiant children who got attention by making trouble and taking the blame for all the family's problems.

The Clown or Jokester: Good-Time Charlie

Charlie was a technical draftsman for an architectural firm where he was "everybody's friend." He cracked jokes in meetings, made people laugh when the firm was under stress, wrote clever memos, made fun of bosses, and routed irreverent cartoons through the interoffice mail. The more stressful things got, the more outrageous his humor became. The spot he'd carved out for himself was Class Clown.

He couldn't understand why people backed away from him when they wanted to get things done and why he was always passed over for promotions. "Nobody takes me seriously," he complained to me.

Charlie had been the third child and taken on the Clown identity in his family. He was the colorful cutup and entertainer, the cheerleader who eased tension in his family by jollying people up and trying to make them feel better. "We can make it, we can do it!" was his theme. Playing this part had distinguished him from the rest of his serious, solemn, academic family and given him a separate, distinct identity that was quite different from his brothers' and sisters'.

When Charlie brought this habit to work and used it to establish an identity at the firm, it got him into trouble. He did relieve stress with his clowning and humor, but he got stuck in that role and used it to the exclusion of other parts of his personality. He was right when he said that nobody took him seriously. They thought of him as good old Charlie and shook their heads, so that despite being an excellent draftsman, he never got ahead.

People who use humor and distraction to create a niche at work run the risk of being considered immature and dismissed as shallow. They may do their coworkers a service by dissipating surface tension, but they often hold themselves back.

The Quiet "Good" Child: Disappearing into the Woodwork

People who are so quiet, cooperative, and withdrawn that they disappear into the woodwork get attention and recognition in two ways. First, everybody notices their absence and starts asking where they are ("Oh, my God, where's Allison!?"). Second, they get strokes for being the "Good" Children who can be counted on not to add any extra stress to an already tense situation. This role is sometimes called the Lost Child, who can always be found in his room staying out of trouble. "At least we can count on him to keep going and get his work done, no matter what's happening," people say.

Suzie was a graphic designer at a firm where people worked in teams on major projects and deadlines. She found being on a team desperately uncomfortable. Rather than participate, she disappeared and handled the small, routine, everyday jobs that could be done alone—so she never got to work on big, exciting projects. "When everyone gets stressed out and there's all that pressure, I just want to crawl under the carpet and not make things worse," she told me. The others stopped asking her to be a part of important projects, and her career was going nowhere.

Suzie was the fourth child in a big, noisy family of seven children, and she got lost in the shuffle. In our sessions, she saw that, ironically, her silence and absence were the only things for which she got attention from her parents and siblings. When they were all getting ready to leave the house, the last minute crisis was always: "What happened to Suzie?! Where *is* she? Is she all right?!"

The night her older unmarried sister announced she was pregnant and the family exploded into chaos, Suzie withdrew to the kitchen, did all the dishes, and cleaned up. Later, her distraught mother found her there and fell into her arms, sobbing, "You're my good daughter. I can always count on you." Being "the good girl who never caused any problems" was Suzie's claim to fame, the identity that distinguished her from all her other siblings.

This habit of withdrawing into the woodwork was no longer working for Suzie. Instead of reducing the stress of a noisy, chaotic workplace, it was actually making her more tense. Her career was stalled, and she was becoming increasingly alienated from the people at work. Suzie began working through the Six Action Steps for Change and gradually participating in larger projects as she could manage them.

People who get attention by disappearing in times of stress often learned early in life not to rock the boat. They were told that children were to be seen and not heard—but they were neither seen *nor* heard. They learned not to cause trouble or contribute to the family's stress. Parents often say of them, "She was always so good and quiet. She'd just go into her room and play by herself."

At work, these people often avoid personal interactions and share very little of the office social life. They are self-sufficient and work well independently, but they often feel alienated, lonely, and angry. Because they are so detached, they are often keen observers of the office emotional dynamics. If you want to know what's really going on in a workplace, ask the Quiet "Good" Child.

◙   If you use these roles or others to carve out a niche for yourself, you can use the Six Action Steps for Change to transform those patterns and start competing in more healthy and productive ways.

◙   QUESTIONS TO ASK YOURSELF

Most of us wind up competing at some point and react to that stress with defensive strategies we learned as children. Ask yourself these questions, then use your answers to complete the exercises in Part 3.

• With whom do you feel competitive at work?

• How do you feel and act around this person?

• What tactics does this person use? What place does he or she try to carve out?

• What place do you carve out for yourself? Superachiever? "Bad" Child? Jokester? Quiet "Good" Child?

• Is there another role, not mentioned here, that you adopt in response to competition at work?

• What place did you carve out for yourself in your family?

7

Do as I Say, Not as I Do:
Mixed Messages

When you were hired, your boss patted you on the back and beamed, "Let me know right away if you have any problems! My door is always open!"

Six months later, your place of work has turned out to be less than the corporate nirvana it had promised to be. Important written and verbal communications don't get delivered. Everybody seems to have hidden agendas and secret strategies for "getting theirs." You regularly receive inaccurate information that fouls up your own work. Nobody will talk to you about these problems.

You schedule a meeting with the boss to straighten things out, but as soon as you start talking, he starts frowning. After a few minutes, he's fidgeting, looking at the clock, rearranging his desk, and scowling. When you ask if something is wrong, he barks, "I don't like to be bothered with details like this. I expect my people to work out the small stuff themselves."

You were set up. You were given one set of instructions and discovered that the actual expectation was something entirely different. What do you do? Skulk away feeling inept and demeaned? Jump onto your boss's desk, grab his tie, and start screaming? Or do you simply give up and stop trying to do a good job because it's a losing battle when the rules keep changing and you never really know what's going on?

In this chapter, we will examine how the invisible rules at work can trigger the same behavior we used to deal with the invisible rules in our families. Invisible rules are as inherent a part of the emotional systems of families and organizations as the roles people play. However, unlike roles, which tend to prescribe who does what under stress, rules focus more on attempting to avoid, deny, or minimize any emotional stress from the outset. As you read, be aware of what you do when you receive mixed messages, and how that behavior reflects what may have happened in your family.

▣ MIXING A MESSAGE

Mixed messages are communications that say one thing and mean another. They often reflect a company's invisible rules. Here are some common corporate mixed messages, with the official policy stated first and the unstated part of the invisible rule in parentheses:

- We reward our employees (*if they're male*).

- Raises are based on achievement (*if you play politics with the right people*).

- We obey the rules and produce top quality (*but will fire whistle-blowers*).

- Be original and creative (*but only within the comfort level of top managers*).

- Everybody here works as a team (*but watch your back because the competition is ruthless and everybody's trying to get ahead*).

- Each work team gets to make its own decisions (*as long as they choose the option that management suggests*).

Most companies give at least some mixed messages. These deceptions may be deliberate attempts to dupe people or simply misguided efforts to bolster the company's image, keep people from getting upset, or mask stress. For instance, a company that's in trouble may protect employees by saying, "We're in fine shape; there's no cause for concern." If people sense the truth, as they usually do, then this mixed message may create even more stress.

In my practice and my work with organizations, I've seen that mixed messages almost always trigger family patterns of behavior for two reasons: First, it is inherently stressful to hear a message that is in conflict with what you know to be true, or to hear one message when you know that quite another message is intended. Second, unclear, contradictory communications abound in most families, so mixed messages can make us feel right at home, as if we're eight years old and listening to our families' mixed messages ("Do as I say, not as I do," or "Everything is just fine" when the family is falling apart).

As children, we needed to fit in and get along, so we often ignored the internal radar that told us we weren't hearing the truth. Instead, most of us either shut down emotionally and got very quiet or else acted out in some way to express our frustration, confusion, and sense of betrayal. Today, when stated policies don't match what actually happens at work, we may have some of those same feelings—and our reactions may be remarkably similar. Most people react in one of two ways:

1. *They fight the system,* sometimes jeopardizing their jobs with reactions ranging from simply calling someone on a contradiction, to taking on the role of self-appointed internal watchdog, to becoming a chronic troublemaker, to quitting or getting fired.

2. *They avoid conflict by capitulating and living with the contradictions.* People's attitudes toward living with the lies can range from resignation to demoralized defeat.

Mixed messages in an organization usually mean mixed messages on a personal level as well—and this is where emotions flare, feelings get hurt, and the chain reaction of family patterns begins. It's one thing for United Technocrats, Inc. to tell you a corporate lie; it's more difficult when your boss John, whom you like and trust and who may hold the key to your future, starts telling you things that you know aren't true or subtly punishing you for disobeying an unwritten rule.

Fighting the System

Kay was thrilled when she landed a technical writing job at a small software company that had a reputation for being employee-friendly and providing both a relaxed atmosphere and phenomenal benefits. "If you're taking care of yourself and your life with benefits like our fitness center, you'll do better work," her boss Jim said during a tour of the beautiful grounds and elaborate facilities.

Kay worked out on the Lifecycle the next week, but only two other people were in the gym at lunch hour. "We don't have time," a coworker later said smugly. "You're lucky you can fit it in." In fact, they all seemed to spend their lunch hours, breaks, and even weekends working. Kay was getting an unspoken message at odds with what Jim had told her: This company is extremely competitive; if you don't give 100 percent every day, you're not a player.

When Kay couldn't take on a big assignment because the family was going out of town that weekend, Jim said, "Well, that's your choice. You have to take care of yourself." Kay sensed she'd just been moved from the A team to the B team.

Her resentment came out in bursts of sarcasm that upset her coworkers, who were still trying to live with the mixed messages. No one wanted to be around someone who brought uncomfortable truths to the surface. The only question was which would come first: Kay's resignation or her pink slip. She quit in a blaze of glory, making a scene with the company president in the lavish employee cafeteria and telling him just what she thought of his "employee-friendly" organization.

Kay told me she had always been "a crusader" who slashed away at the mixed messages in her socially prominent family. Her father was a New York financier whose wife ignored his many affairs and unscrupulous business dealings and maintained a smooth, cool facade even when he abused her physically. Kay insisted on bringing up ugly truths at the dinner table, but everyone pretended not to hear her. When she was eighteen, she left a letter castigating them for their lies, moved out, and hadn't seen any of them since that day.

"It was my way of winning," she told me. "I couldn't beat them on their own turf, so I showed them I could play on a whole different field, a better one than theirs." Telling the truth, making a dramatic exit, and burning her bridges were the only ways Kay knew to express her frustration—and she had done the same thing at the software company.

As she worked through the Six Action Steps for Change in Part 3, Kay saw just what her pattern had cost her and how to change it.

People who respond to mixed messages by fighting the system are often so angry, upset, resentful, or confused that they don't communicate effectively. Their antagonistic "I'm right and you're wrong" attitude isn't usually productive. They become known as troublemakers, which creates more stress—both for them and for their organizations. They often keep fighting losing battles until they either get fired or quit.

Living with the Lies

In the face of mixed messages, some people simply give up on trying to sort out the contradictions and stop trying to do a good job. They stay physically, but leave emotionally.

My client Paul was excited about being on the cutting edge of American business when he landed a position at an electronics-parts manufacturer. The company claimed to be a leader in both participatory, team-based management and Total Quality Management, the system that permits no mistakes or defects and demands continuous improvement in its constant quest for perfection.

After a few months, he realized that participatory management and the team concept meant that management brought ideas to the teams and asked for their input—but expected them to be rubber-stamped. The official policy was: We want you to be involved. The reality was: We want you involved, but only as long as we still have control.

"It's a joke," Paul said. "They tell us they want us to participate, and then they tell us what to decide."

His frustration deepened when he began to see how Total Quality Management (TQM) worked. The party line was: We are constantly improving on an already perfect product; no one makes mistakes. In reality, some of the company's work was shoddy, and many important things fell through the cracks.

Paul would sit at lunch with the other assistant managers, listening in disbelief as they talked up the company, the team concept, and TQM. His boss was one of the biggest cheerleaders, brushing Paul off when he suggested that there were problems and giving him the clear, if unspoken, message: Play on the team—or don't play.

Paul considered quitting, but the job and the money were too good. He decided to live with his disappointment and just numbed out. He showed up and did his work, but he had no enthusiasm and lost his creative edge. He feigned excitement, but underneath he never really shook that feeling of defeat and capitulation.

This was just how Paul had reacted to the mixed messages in his family. Nothing terrible had happened in his home. No one had come home drunk or thrown frying pans across the living room, but no one was very happy, either. His father worked all the time, his parents were unhappy together but resigned to their marriage, his mother watched television and took "muscle relaxants," and his older sister spent as much time as she could out of the house.

"We're very lucky to have such a happy, wonderful family, and you children are lucky to be growing up in a loving environment," his mother would say tightly over Sunday dinner. Paul and his sister would stare into space, knowing that they were no match for their parents' delusions or outright lies. Paul's sister told him when she was ten and he was eight, "You just have to keep quiet until you're eighteen. Then you can leave and never come back." He did just that, and now he was doing the same thing at the electronics company—keeping quiet until he was sixty-five, then leaving.

Mixed messages occur in every family, so we are all at risk to react with defensive strategies we learned as children. Chapter 10 gives specific techniques for clarifying mixed messages. For now, the important thing is to get in touch with how you are likely to react to them.

◙ QUESTIONS TO ASK YOURSELF

Answer these questions to start exploring your reactions to mixed messages:

• What are the three most jarring mixed messages in your company?

• What are the unwritten rules that nobody talks about but everybody must follow?

• How do you feel when you have to operate within this system?

• How do you react to mixed messages? Are you more likely to fight or to shut down and numb out? Do you have another, entirely different reaction?

• What were the mixed messages in your family?

• How did you deal with them?

8

One-Upmanship: Covert Power Games

Y ou are hard at work when a coworker who had heard you're up for a promotion leans over your shoulder, peers at your computer screen, and says smugly, "Still working on *that,* huh?" He slaps you on the back and laughs. "Good luck!" Then he turns on his heel and is gone.

You're confused and mildly offended. You're not sure exactly what he meant, but you don't think you like it and feel at a slight disadvantage the next time you see him.

You have just been the object of sarcasm, one of the many covert power games that are often used to deal with unexpressed and unresolved emotional desires at work. These games of emotional one-upmanship are really attempts to manipulate, control, or change how you think, feel, and act so the game player gets to feel better about him- or herself.

We have numerous ways of relating available to us in our work relationships. Some are effective and appropriate, such as negotiating, conflict resolution, and assertiveness; others are manipulative and destructive. Covert power games involving one-upmanship fall into this latter category and are usually the most difficult to identify and deal with. We'll primarily explore these in this chapter, as they encompass the broadest array of ineffective stress-induced behavior.

Like invisible roles and rules, these invisible ways of relating are often automatic reactions that we learned as children, and for which we reach instinctively when we feel stressed or threatened. It can be uncomfortable to explore which power games you use, but understanding when and with whom you're most likely to play emotional one-upmanship is the first step in making changes.

◨ HOW POWER GAMES WORK

People play covert power games when they are afraid they have no power or are losing what power they do have. The need to put others down usually comes from feeling unworthy or "less than." Power games are often covert because people don't want to be caught playing them.

Some of the power games we will discuss in this chapter are: innuendo and indirect criticism, withholding important information, threats, bullying, intimidation, shame, ridicule, the silent treatment, emotional bribery, patronizing, and condescension.

Covert power games transcend the office pecking order. They can be used on people above, below, or at the same level as the game player on the organizational chart. One client of mine had an employee come up to her at an office party and say, "You're a great boss, just like my third grade teacher, Sister Mary Margaret. She really whipped our multiplication tables into us." It was technically a compliment, but it made my client sound like a dictator.

We often play covert power games as a reaction to someone playing them on us. This kind of retaliation, conscious or unconscious, only escalates the battle and damages our self esteem. All covert power games depend for their success on the people at whom they are directed. If you don't bite—if you refuse to be humiliated or manipulated, or to change your behavior to suit the other person, then the game can backfire and make the other player look childish and mean-spirited. Of course, the key to not biting is understanding when you most want to bite.

Covert power games can be nasty, and it's easy to criticize people who play them—including ourselves—but that leaves us powerless and only creates more stress. The best strategy is to understand that people play these games because they feel insecure, powerless, and stressed; to recognize our own power-game proclivities; and to take the steps outlined in Part 3 for letting go of them and finding healthier ways of relating to people at work.

As you read, note which power games were played in your family and which you may be playing now.

Innuendo and Indirect Criticism

Innuendo and indirect criticism are used to diminish another person's self-esteem or position in the organization by hinting, without actually saying, negative things about him or her. They often take the form of snide or sarcastic remarks that cast doubt on the person's character or performance without making specific accusations that the person can refute.

- "She's a wonderful mother. If little Adrienne is sick, she drops whatever she's doing and rushes home."

- "We'll keep him around forever to deal with our older customers."

- "Dawn's spelling and punctuation are perfect. I wish the rest of her reports made as much sense."

These kinds of comments are often disguised as jokes or asides so that if anyone objects, the game player can say, "Can't you take a joke? I was just kidding. You're so sensitive!"

Innuendo and indirect criticism can be made directly to the other person, to his or her boss, to coworkers, to his or her staff—or to all of the above, as in the example that follows. Mort felt that Charlene was stealing his thunder and said sarcastically to her, when he saw her leaving early one day, "Boy, you're really working hard this week." Later, he "casually" mentioned to their boss, Bonnie, "I guess I can get that information from Charlene tomorrow if she comes in." To her staff, he said, "You guys have it easy, working for Charlene. Don't tell *my* secretary you have such a cushy setup."

People who use innuendo and indirect criticism often have a horror of getting caught, and Mort had chosen the wrong person with whom to play these particular games. Charlene was a direct, assertive person who was sensitive to office politics, and his sarcastic comment to her tipped her off. The next day, she told him she didn't like his implication and if he had anything to say to her, he should say it directly. She asked if he'd talked to anyone else about her and even though he said he hadn't, he knew that she knew he had.

It was Mort's worst nightmare come true. Instead of Charlene's looking unprofessional and incompetent, he felt like an immature jerk and was sure she'd find a way to make him look bad with the others. This wasn't the first time innuendo had backfired on Mort, and he came to see me because he didn't understand why he kept engaging in this power game.

In our sessions, Mort saw that he came from a "perfect" family in which nobody could criticize or confront one another. The only way to communicate that something was wrong was in a backhanded way, which usually involved innuendo. Instead of saying, "Mom, I think Suzie took my bat," he learned to say, "Mom, my bat is missing. I guess I'll ask Suzie about it because she was here when it disappeared. Maybe she saw someone take it before she left for her game."

Mort knew that this way of relating didn't work in the adult professional world, and his experience with Charlene made him ready to do something about it. He learned to stop and think whenever he was upset with or jealous of someone, because those were the stressful circumstances that triggered this old family pattern. He made it a rule not to talk about those people to third parties, and either to speak directly to them about the problem or else handle it within himself. Mort slipped "off the wagon" occasionally, but as he developed the new habit of communicating directly and started to experience its benefits, he actually came to prefer this more direct and aboveboard style of dealing with stress in relationships.

Intentionally Withholding Information

Information is power, especially in professional settings. Intentionally withholding information can make another person appear weak, stupid, incompetent, or uninterested in the job. This power game is silent and sometimes goes unnoticed because it involves *not* doing something.

Denise's secretary, Evelyn, confided to her that she'd heard via the company's informal but powerful support staff information network (SSIN, as the group liked to call itself) that the district manager would be paying a surprise visit to their office on Friday. Denise got ahead with her work, cleaned up her desk, dressed well—and didn't tell her colleague and "pal" Howard, who showed up late, disheveled, and apparently unconcerned about all the messy, unfinished work on his desk. When the district manager arrived, Denise was gracious, available, on top of everything, and appeared to be doing both of their jobs. Howard looked like an incompetent slacker who was trying to ride on Denise's coattails.

Evelyn wasn't the only SSIN member who talked to people outside the network, and Howard soon found out exactly what had happened. He ended his friendship with Denise and had only the most minimum and necessary contact with her. This not only handicapped her work but was devastating personally. Denise learned that in winning a covert power game, she had actually lost.

When she came to see me, we discovered that withholding important information had been her family's *modus operandi*. She and her sister were highly competitive and often used the tactic of withholding information. This dynamic took many forms—not giving each other messages from their mother about chores, not delivering messages from boys—and was always used to gain an advantage or to make the other girl look bad.

The loss of her personal and professional friendship with Howard made Denise realize what this tactic was costing her. Once she became aware that withholding information was a habit she'd developed as a child to get ahead, she used the exercises in Part 3 to change her behavior. She developed cues and reminders that helped her pass along information to the appropriate people and started catching herself withholding as she became more aware of that childhood pattern.

Withholding information is a classic family dynamic, and most of us are at risk for it. Parents regularly withhold important information from children to "spare their feelings" or because "they aren't old enough to understand" things like marital difficulties, affairs, addictions, severe financial problems, disputes over Grandpa's will, a gay uncle, or an ancestor of a different race. Children almost always pick up on an intuitive level that something is wrong or being withheld, and the anxiety and confusion they feel is often much worse than having to deal with the information they "can't handle."

When you play this particular power game, you're likely to get caught. It's usually not difficult for the person who's been denied information to trace back through the lines of communication and find out who the withheld information *should* have come from.

Threats, Bullying, and Intimidation

Phyllis worked on commission in cosmetics at a large department store where she and her colleagues called one another "sales sharks." They swam around, waiting for one another to leave customers for a second, then swooped in to steal the sale. Their competition was laced with threats, bullying, and intimidation.

"I'll beat you today," Phyllis's nemesis Tina would threaten. "I'll get two of yours, and you'd better stay away from mine." Stiff smiles accompanied the banter. People knew it was sort of a joke, sort of not. When one of them did steal a sale, there were terrible fights and weeks of silence. Phyllis was tired, frustrated, and stressed out, but she couldn't bring herself to quit—and that's why she came to see me.

We discovered that Phyllis's family situation was a lot like the cosmetics counter. Her four brothers and one sister were wildly competitive and had almost no supervision. Both parents worked and felt overwhelmed by the children's separate "family" and the chaos that reigned in it. Phyllis grew up in a world of fistfights, yelling, and domination by whoever was most forceful that day.

The sharks at the cosmetics counter were nothing compared to her brothers. Under the stress of competition, she jumped right in, using the only weapons she knew. But after two years there, she wasn't sure she wanted to spend the rest of her life as an emotional gladiator and was willing to make drastic changes in order to get some peace, quiet, and serenity in her professional life. Using the guidelines in Part 3, she got transferred to another department where the competition wasn't as fierce and used the techniques in Chapter 10 to disengage from power games and start developing more supportive relationships with her coworkers.

Threats, bullying, and intimidation are a way of life in many families, so many of us learn these tactics at an early age. Parents use these strategies to make children obey, siblings use them to manipulate one another, and children use them to control their parents when they say such things as:

- "Dad won't like it if you don't let me practice shooting baskets, Mom."

- "If you ever do that again, I'll run away and you'll never see me again."

- "If you were as strict as Sally's parents about curfews, I'd kill myself."

Most of us have been on both the giving and receiving ends of threats and intimidation in our families. It's not surprising that these behaviors often appear at work.

Shame and Ridicule

Shame and ridicule are used to coerce others into doing what the game player wants by making them feel bad about themselves unless they do, and also to get back at or humiliate someone around whom the game player feels resentful or inferior. They show up in such comments as:

+ "Late again? I'm going to start telling you things are due three days before they actually are, just like I do with my kids."

+ "If you can't handle the project, Janice can."

Bob resented his manager because he didn't think the man was very good at what he did and had been promoted because of ties between his family and the company president's family. The manager had gone to West Point and been in the army, but Bob figured he must have left the service because he was incompetent. One morning after a difficult meeting, Bob heard himself say to this man, "You used to be a major, and I wasn't even in the army, but look how well I've done here."

Bob was embarrassed even before the words were out of his mouth. It was a childish thing to say and he knew it, but somehow he hadn't been able to help himself. The resentment he felt toward this man and the stress it produced put him on "automatic."

After we'd talked about his family, Bob recognized that it was just the kind of jab his father always took at Bob and his brother John. He told John, who had trouble in school, "When I was your age, I knew twice that much math." Bob didn't make the football team and was asked sarcastically, "Now that you can't make it with the big guys, are you going to join the debate team?"

Bob and John learned to salve their egos by shaming and ridiculing each other. It was how they learned to deal with hurt and resentment and how Bob was reacting with his manager until he started taking the Six Action Steps for Change in Part 3.

Shame and ridicule are standard family dynamics. Parents use them to control children's behavior with such comments as:

+ "What kind of a haircut is that?"

+ "You look ridiculous in a skirt that short."

+ "You were always selfish, ever since you were little. We always said that about her, didn't we, Charlie?"

Children, in turn, learn to use these tactics on their parents and on one another. They are automatic reactions to feeling threatened, and so it's not surprising that, years later, they make their way to the office.

The Silent Treatment

It's no fun to be ignored, and it's difficult to resolve problems when people don't talk. The silent treatment affects both well-being and job performance. It produces a powerless feeling, and that's just what the game player intends.

Jean designed furniture for a small crafts company with only ten employees and found herself engaged in a Ping-Pong match of silent treatments. All the creative people were contemptuous of the highly paid "bean-counting" business manager, Vance. They thought Vance secretly wanted to fire most of them to cut down on salaries. Jean's reaction was to give Vance the silent treatment. She never spoke to him except when it was absolutely necessary and ignored him when they passed in the hall.

Jean was a favorite of the elderly owner, and her job seemed relatively secure until the day they found out that some staff would have to be cut and that Vance was in charge of deciding who would go. Jean wished she could take back her silence, but the silent treatment doesn't work that way. When people are shut out, they often feel so hurt and disempowered that they are wary of reconciling.

Vance turned the tables on Jean when the power shifted to him, and gave *her* the silent treatment. She tried to make him talk to her, but he refused to respond to her increasingly agitated questions with anything beyond monosyllables. She finally threw herself on the mercy of the owner, but by that time she looked—and was—hysterical. Sure enough, she was number one on Vance's hit list.

Jean's father had reacted to anything upsetting in the family—from dinner not being ready on time to her brother's drunk driving charge— with stony silence. He had held all the power in the family, and so his was the behavior she imitated when she felt the stress of powerlessness and wanted to feel more in control. This behavior hadn't been very productive in Jean's family—she had *looked* in control, but not felt that way—and it was disastrous in business.

The silent treatment is one of the most commonly used covert power games for four reasons:

1. *It is a passive game,* relatively easy to play because it involves *not* doing something, rather than doing something.

2. *It can go unnoticed,* except by the people on whom it is used, because it's not as belligerent or obviously troublesome as, for instance, threats and intimidation.

3. *Withdrawing is a common response to stress,* and the silent treatment is a natural power game for those who want to avoid confrontation or direct communication.

4. *It is played almost universally in families* and is part of most people's emotional baggage. Very few people were not subjected to some form of silent treatment when they were children. Consider, for example, the following characterizations: (a) a martyred mother who retreated into silence as punishment when she didn't get what she wanted; (b) a stoic, distant father who seemed not to know or care what was going on in the family; (c) angry parents who inspired fear by looking as if they were about to explode, but said nothing.

Most of us either play this power game ourselves or were subjected to it at some point. Notice when, and with whom, you are most likely to use the silent treatment as a defense.

Emotional Bribery

Emotional bribery is making someone feel guilty or otherwise uncomfortable unless they do what you want.

There are two kinds of emotional bribery: positive and negative. Positive bribery is a carrot; you stroke the person or offer him some other inducement to do what you want. Negative bribery is a stick; you threaten to punish him, blame him, or withhold something if he doesn't do what you want.

Matt was a sales manager who had been sizing up his sales staff, Wes and Betty, for a year and was a master of emotional bribery. When the company experienced a slump and Matt was told to increase sales by 25 percent, he used two different tactics with them. Betty was subjected to negative emotional bribery when Matt said, "I'm really in trouble here. Unless you guys come up with this increase, I'll get fired." Betty rushed back to her desk in a panic that she was now responsible for Matt keeping his job.

Wes got positive emotional bribery. Matt spoke to him as a peer and confidant, saying, "You're the guy I can rely on, my best salesman. I know you'll get those numbers for me, and we'll celebrate at Ernie's." The implicit message in this "positive" form of emotional bribery is: "Doing this will make me approve of and care about you" (and "not doing this will make me disapprove of and not care about you").

Betty and Wes scurried away, determined for different reasons to produce results—but they didn't make many sales. They were both doing it for Matt, not for themselves, and both felt somewhat manipulated and resentful.

Matt's family had been a miasma of emotional bribery. His parents had used both positive and negative bribery to manipulate him into good grades (Father: "You're my guy, Matt; I can count on the number-one son to get all A's"), good behavior (Mother: "It would break my heart if you turned out like your cousin David"), and even a good marriage (Mother: "She's the kind of girl you'll be proud of; that Naomi was just a flash in the pan"). Once Matt was aware of his tendency to use emotional bribery and clearer about the negative results it produced, he could start letting go, using the techniques in Chapter 10.

Emotional bribes are legal tender in most families. Parents bribe their children with candy, postponement of bedtime, extended television viewing, sleepovers with friends, mall time, etc. As children get older, they can be bribed with approval, favoritism over other siblings, and even inheritances. A mother can say, "I'd just hate to see your father's hard-earned money fall into that woman's hands. Whatever happened to that sweet little Melanie you were seeing last summer?"

Children control things their parents want as well and often bribe them with such prizes as good behavior, good grades, appropriate choices in dating and marriage partners, the ability to produce grand-children, and, as the parents get older, financial security.

Many people grow up assuming that emotional bribery is a normal part of human interaction and don't think twice about bringing it to work. In fact, it is a conditioned reaction to stressful situations that we learned in our families. We're just dealing in promotions instead of candy bars and raises instead of relaxed curfews. As with all covert power games, you can make immediate improvements using the techniques in Chapter 10 and deeper changes using the exercises in Part 3.

◘ PATRONIZING AND CONDESCENSION

These power games imply that the game player is speaking from a superior or more experienced position to a lesser, weaker, or more in-experienced inferior—in tones that are either drippingly kind or semi-sarcastic.

Jill had been the only woman vice president for six years when Carla was named vice president for operations. Suddenly, Carla got all the at-tention, and Jill felt ignored and threatened. Her unique position was gone, and she reacted to this stress by adopting a patronizing attitude toward Carla. She implied that Carla had a lot to learn, that the atten-tion would pass, and that in the end everyone would see that Jill was more important with such comments as:

• "You guys acted this same way at Don's surprise party when that hooker jumped out of the cake."

• "Enjoy it while you can, Carla. We'll get down to business Monday, and you'll see what it's like at the top."

It was a tactic she had seen her father use when her brother Mick started to mature and get attention from women. The father would im-ply that Mick was really just a boy with jabs like, "Did you shave this week, kid?" Mick threatened Jill's position in the family as well when their mother started giving him more and more attention, and Jill adopted her father's tactic to cut Mick down and salve her ego with such comments as, "What are all those girls going to think when you flunk math and don't graduate? Anything I can do to help?" When Carla made vice president and posed a similar threat to her position, she instinctively reached for the tactics that had stopped the pain when she was a teen.

Condescension and patronizing are tactics used between parents, among siblings, and between parents and children. You often see them applied by one parent to the child of the same sex whose strength, beauty, intelligence, masculinity, or femininity may feel threatening to the parent:

- (*Mother to daughter*) "When you lose that baby fat and we can get you into some decent clothes, I'm sure somebody will ask you out."

- (*Father to son*) "That's a good report card, but there's more to being a man than bringing home A's."

When you know how condescending and patronizing were used in your family and how you are likely to use them, then you are back in control. You can make choices, rather than falling into ineffective knee-jerk reactions.

◘ HOW TO TELL WHEN YOU'RE PLAYING COVERT POWER GAMES

Power games do not stand alone; they are one dimension in how members of any emotional system can relate. In work environments where emotional openness is seen as nonproductive or, worse yet, a sign of weakness and incompetence, covert power games abound. The following Six Signs of Defensiveness usually indicate that you're jumping into a mode of behavior that provides a short-term sense of being one up at the expense of your long-term self-esteem and emotional well-being:

1. *High emotional charge*: being overly expressive or reactive ("What do you mean by that?!") and losing your sense of humor

2. *Rigid thinking*: needing to be right and to have the last word

3. *Teaching and preaching*: endless explaining, telling everyone exactly what's going on and what they should be doing

4. *Blaming, ridiculing, or criticizing others* and being unwilling to be responsible for your own mistakes

5. *Pretending to be confused or stupid*—the defiant "I don't know" shrug

6. *Cynicism or sarcasm* to distance yourself and appear superior.

□ QUESTIONS TO ASK YOURSELF

To start discovering what covert power games you may be playing, ask yourself these questions:

• Which of these games feels most familiar: innuendo and indirect criticism, withholding important information, threats, bullying, intimidation, shame, ridicule, the silent treatment, emotional bribery, patronizing, or condescension?

• Do you play other covert power games not mentioned in this chapter?

• With what kinds of people do you find yourself playing these covert power games? In what circumstances?

• Which covert power games were played in your family?

• Who played them?

9

This Family Has No Problems: Denial, Avoidance, and Self-Deception

Your boss hired Lynn to help with the overload in your department. He hated the hiring process and picked her because she was the best he'd seen after three interviews. Now it turns out that she can't do the work and isn't pulling her weight. You and two colleagues tell the boss that having Lynn doesn't help and actually consumes more of your time, but he won't listen.

"Look, it's my department and I'll hire who I want," he says defensively. "Things are getting done. If we have a problem, I'll do something about it." He ignores the fact that things are getting done because you're doing them and refuses to hear your message about Lynn because then he might have to start the hiring process again.

People who deny or avoid problems waste time wishing, hoping, and pretending that uncomfortable situations don't exist so that they don't have to deal with them or feel the stressful emotions that they engender. This behavior not only feeds the system's tendency to maintain the current patterns, it also provides a breeding ground for the one-upmanship behavior discussed in the previous chapter.

I've seen in my practice and my work with organizations that denial, avoidance, and self-deception occur at both an individual and a corporate level. These invisible ways of relating are part of every family's dynamic, and we often learned as children to try minimizing stress by pretending that the stressful situation or relationship simply wasn't there. As we noted in Chapter 2, most companies encourage people to stuff, deny, or avoid negative emotions and are not eager to discuss problems in the organization as a whole.

▣ HOW DENIAL, AVOIDANCE, AND SELF-DECEPTION WORK

Denial, avoidance, and self-deception are natural human strategies for managing information that might overload us with stress or anxiety. If we think a piece of information might produce too much stress, we simply ignore or avoid it. The trouble starts when we use this strategy all the time and problems never get solved because we can't admit they exist. When that pattern begins, the situation cannot get better and will probably get worse.

There are subtle differences among denial, avoidance, and self-deception:

• *Denial* is refusing to accept that there is a problem. It's the company that won't believe it can no longer afford expensive offices and a staff of two hundred; the family that says, "Our child doesn't have a drug problem"; the individual who says, "My job is getting done. Some people just complain about everything."

• *Avoidance* is refusing to deal with the problem, even though it has become obvious. The company can't meet its payroll but keeps telling people, "Give us a week, a month, and everything will be fine." The family won't discuss the situation, even though the child is now in jail. The individual says, "Nobody could have finished that project on time. Sally just has it in for me."

• *Self-deception* is seeing fault only in others and refusing to be responsible for one's own part in the situation. The CEO of the failed company says, "They never told me that things were that bad." The family says, "Her friends at school turned her on to drugs; we had nothing to do with it." The individual says, "They didn't fire me; I really quit because I couldn't stand working with Sally."

If your job is in jeopardy, you may *deny* for some time that the company would ever let you go. Even when you realize that your position will be phased out, you may *avoid* talking about it or looking for a new job. *Self-deception* may come into play if you insist that the job had been essential to the organization but that corporate sharks were out to get you.

We can't count on changing how companies operate, but we do have control over our own reactions, and over whether we use our own energy to deny or avoid problems or to engage and handle them directly. This chapter will help you identify how denial, avoidance, and self-deception were used in your family, and when and how you may be using them now. As you read, think about the times when denying or avoiding a person or problem may actually have caused you more trouble and stress.

Denying Damages

Rennie ran her small management consulting firm with smoke, mirrors, and charm. She was an extremely engaging person who, in the first year of business, rarely left a sales call without a commitment to one of her corporate workshops and a big check. Her problem was follow-through. She had trouble with scheduling, organizing, and presenting the material—and in fact didn't have much to say. Word got out that Rennie didn't deliver an effective product, and sales slowed to a halt.

Her business manager told her she needed to stop making these razzle-dazzle sales calls, develop some serious material, and organize the company to deliver it—but Rennie only wanted to hear praise and good news. "I'm the heart of this company," she said. "If I'm having fun, we'll succeed." She refused to admit that there was a problem. Her world was filled with sunshine, and she was going to keep it that way at any cost. The price turned out to be her company, which folded at the end of the second year.

When Rennie and I talked, we saw that she had learned about denial from her mother, who was the original sunshine girl and never let the children express sadness, anger, or concern about problems. Mind over matter was her motto, and the children were expected to keep smiling even during the year Rennie's brother was caught at school with drugs and Rennie was involved in a serious car accident that left her hospitalized for two months. If the children brought up unpleasant feelings, they were punished by silence and being ignored.

Rennie had trouble breaking the pattern of denying that problems existed because much of her identity was based on being sunny and charming at all times. She had to do the exercises in Part 3 scrupulously in order to make changes. She told me that it was worth the effort, however, because she is a person of more substance now. People take her, and her new business, more seriously.

Avoiding Anxiety

Tim had worked hard to develop a commission package that he insisted promoted teamwork among the sales staff at his real estate company. When Gail came on board from a larger, more sophisticated company, she pointed out flaws in the commission package and made some suggestions based on what they'd done at her old company.

Tim didn't want to hear it. He'd had several complaints from salespeople about the plan and he respected Gail's opinion, but the process of developing it had been so grueling that he was simply unwilling to repeat it—and so he tried avoiding the problem by refusing to hear what Gail had to say. "Look," he told her, "I put a lot of time and energy into this plan, and I'm not changing it." The results were disastrous. Over the next year, he lost six key people as a result of the package and his attitude toward it.

When I asked Tim if anyone in his family had dealt with difficulties in this way, he asked, "You mean Stonewall?" It was what he and his siblings had called their mother, an extremely busy and successful professional woman who raised four children alone and adopted the Scarlett O'Hara approach to problem solving: "I'll think about that tomorrow." Only tomorrow never came for most of these problems.

Tim and the other kids learned that if a situation was too distressing, you just pretended it wasn't there. What they didn't see as children was the anxiety it caused their mother to know on some level that all these problems existed—one kid's bad grades, another beating Tim up regularly, his sister's drug use—and that she wasn't dealing with them. All they knew was that if they brought up problems, they got smacked.

When stress at work triggered this same family pattern of avoidance in Tim, he saw how anxious it made him to live in the middle of a problem he wasn't solving, or even exploring. He also saw the effect on his bottom line.

Scary Self-Deception

Ralph was the chief financial officer for a chain of women's clothing stores that were in serious financial trouble. He blamed the problem completely on marketing and refused to look at the difficulties in his own area: pricing, expensive leases, and operating costs.

"It's not my problem," Ralph would say. "It's them! It's their problem!" His refusal to accept any responsibility began an internal feud that spread throughout the organization.

Ralph had learned early in life to use self-deception as a defense against uncomfortable realities about himself. His father had been an explosive man, successful in business but extremely rigid and tyrannical. He couldn't allow for any imperfection in himself and blamed others whenever anything went wrong in his personal or professional life. He insisted on perfection in all his children—especially in Ralph, who was the oldest boy. The pressure was too much, and Ralph flunked out of prep school. His father told him that was the last time he could ever "screw up." To Ralph, that meant that if he ever made another mistake, he had to find someone else to blame—and he'd been deceiving himself in that way ever since.

As an adult, Ralph said he didn't succeed at jobs because people didn't recognize his talent, or because he got sick and was in the hospital for the big conference, or because his wife wasn't doing all she could for his career—anything to avoid personal responsibility for something that might be considered a failure.

When Ralph recognized this pattern of self-deception as an instinctive reaction to the stress of potential failure, he could start making changes. He explored in detail exactly how it had gotten started and what kept it in place, and used the steps and exercises in Part 3 to break the habit. Ralph didn't transform himself overnight, but he made steady progress and is now seeing the results. He is succeeding in a highly responsible position and having more fun than he's had since he was a kid.

□ HOW CAN YOU TELL WHEN YOU'RE
  STUCK IN DENIAL, AVOIDANCE,
  OR SELF-DECEPTION?

Recognizing these invisible ways of relating can be tricky, because if you're engaging in them, you may already be in a state of self-delusion. Remember that the more these dynamics were used in your family, the more likely you are to react automatically to them now. Four clues that you're stuck in denial, avoidance, or self-deception are:

1. *You feel threatened by new information or new realities.* The information or reality doesn't have to be inherently frightening; it just has to threaten your self-esteem, security, or well-being. A new position in the department or a new organizational structure may actually work to your benefit—but if you perceive them as threatening, you may not be able to accept them and may start operating as if they don't exist.

2. *The feelings associated with an event or situation are too uncomfortable or unpleasant.* Ralph's feeling of failure was simply unacceptable to him, and he was prepared to do anything—even make the situation worse—in order to avoid experiencing it.

3. *You subscribe to the organization's rigid unspoken rules about putting aside feelings in order to get the job done, and deny your emotions.* If the organization says you're not supposed to feel disappointment, fear, or inadequacy and you buy into that program, then you may have to deny the existence of anything that might prompt those feelings.

4. *There is already too much stress on you personally or on your organization, and you can't absorb any more information.* It's possible to be so emotionally overloaded that you just can't take in anything that might cause more tension. When this is the case, denial or avoidance become effective means of managing stress. At some point, however, these mechanisms have to be relaxed so that you don't exist in a state of permanent or chronic denial.

Proceed with extreme caution when you make changes in the organization's patterns of denial and avoidance. People who step up and speak the truth before others are ready to hear it can get into serious trouble. Do the exercises in Part 3 carefully to identify the problem, assess the risks, and learn exactly how to proceed. If you go forward without this preparation, you could jeopardize your job.

◘ QUESTIONS TO ASK YOURSELF

The most powerful things you can do right now is to start thinking about how your family used denial and avoidance and to monitor when you may be tempted to indulge in these self-deceptions. Ask yourself these questions:

• What are the three most uncomfortable relationships for you at work?

• Do you find yourself wishing that these people would quit or get fired before you have to deal seriously with them?

• Do you catch yourself denying that there is a problem with them? Avoiding them? Blaming them?

• Have you considered dealing with the problem directly? How did you feel about that?

• How did denial, avoidance, and self-deception work in your family? What was denied or avoided? Who held the web of deception together? How did you participate?

10

Taking Charge: Thirteen Tools for Claiming Your Power

In Chapters 4–9, you looked at which old family roles, rules, and ways of relating you're most likely to repeat in reaction to stress with people at work.

This chapter answers the question: What do you do instead of those old behaviors? In Part 3, you'll do exercises that show you what changes are possible in your specific situation and how to make them without putting your job at risk. This chapter gives you general suggestions for avoiding knee-jerk defensive reactions and improving relationships at work that you can use before, during, and after you make those specific changes. It is a toolbox of thirteen basic techniques for moving from surviving to thriving. Each technique is followed by a brief reference to the behaviors that it can best help you alter. Though not exhaustive, this summary will facilitate your efforts to change. You can open it up at any time and select the tools best suited to your situation.

These Power Tools free you from the past and open up a whole new world of successful, supportive, and enjoyable relationships.

These new techniques may feel awkward or unnatural at first. Remember, your old ways are ingrained habits and, by now, the path of least resistance. Stick with the new ways until you overcome the initial resistance. Remember why you are using them—to develop relationships that nurture both your well-being and your career.

◙ POWER TOOL #1: PRACTICE "NO-FAULT THINKING"

No-Fault Thinking is the opposite of Faulty Thinking, or blame. It changes the focus from *Who is to blame and what is he doing wrong?* to *What can I do to improve this situation?* You take all the energy you've been putting into assigning fault and direct it toward finding solutions.

Most of us learned as children to point the finger at someone else when we felt defensive, stressed, or panicked. The only acceptable outcome was that *someone or something outside ourselves was to blame,* and we couldn't back down until that became clear to all concerned. The problem with this tactic is that it keeps us stuck. Faulty Thinking is reactive and defensive. In family systems therapy, we've seen that it always leads to reactive blame and more Faulty Thinking.

If you have ever watched two children tease one another until one of them cries, then you have seen how Faulty Thinking works. At some point, one of the children may scream, "Mommy, Mommy, Joey's after me again!" The suggestion is that the whole problem is Joey's fault, but most parents know better. They understand that fights are usually two-way streets and that one child's behavior is influenced by the other's. Both are responsible.

No-Fault Thinking recognizes that everyone has some responsibility for what is happening. Each situation is part of an emotional web in which everybody's thoughts, feelings, and behaviors influence everybody else's. As a No-Fault Thinker, you look at situations in terms of how you may be creating the stress for yourself or letting old family patterns contribute to the difficulty. This gives you the power to change those dynamics.

In the heat of an argument or threatening situation, it may be difficult to step back, see how you fit into what's happening, and accept responsibility for your part in it. To make the transition from Faulty Thinking to No-Fault Thinking, you have to detach from the stress of the moment, give up the need to be right, and think of yourself as a strong, effective person who minimizes casting blame. The key ingredients of No-Fault Thinking are openness, self-responsibility, trust, and flexibility.

The next time you are tempted to defend yourself with Faulty Thinking, stop and ask yourself two questions:

- What do I want the other person to understand about me right now?

- Is the way I'm about to communicate going to help him or her understand that?

If you can honestly answer yes to this question, then you are probably using No-Fault Thinking. Give yourself credit for taking an uncomfortable step, and remember the payoff: more pleasant, productive relationships at work and a quantum leap in self-esteem.

Although No-Fault Thinking is one of the most empowering ways to relate to anyone under any circumstances, it is most beneficial in resolving the following behaviors:

- Covert power games

- The Victim-Persecutor-Rescuer triangle

▣ POWER TOOL #2: BECOME AN OBJECTIVE OBSERVER

The key to No-Fault Thinking is to become an objective observer of situations and relationships at work. You can only recognize family-patterned reactions—in yourself and in others—when you can stay somewhat detached. If you're caught up in your own reaction and flailing around in your office's invisible emotional web, you won't even be able to see the problem clearly, let alone find and implement solutions.

Observing objectively means to become aware of your own thoughts, feelings, and behaviors without judging yourself harshly. It doesn't help to see your old family-patterned behaviors and then beat yourself up. Blaming yourself isn't any more productive than blaming others. Simply notice what you are doing, stop for a moment, and recognize that you have a choice whether or not to continue in that direction.

The more you know about yourself and your own family patterns, the more willing you are to see your own part in the situation, and the more you practice these techniques, the easier it is to step back and observe objectively.

Practice becoming an objective observer by monitoring your reactions in day-to-day situations at work. As you become adept at noticing your reactions but not blaming yourself for them, you'll be able to break the habit and pull yourself out of emotional quagmires more quickly and easily.

The ability to be an objective observer will enable you to better assess the roles you play in your workplace. In particular, this Power Tool will help you identify:

- Rules that you have brought into the workplace from your family

- The roles of Hero, Scapegoat, or Martyr

- Your role in emotional triangles

- The rules of the emotional system of the workplace.

▣ POWER TOOL #3: BE AWARE OF "THE DOOM LOOP"

Even people who are familiar with their own family patterns and adept at noticing them occasionally fall into what I call The Doom Loop. The Doom Loop occurs when you keep engaging in old, defensive, self-destructive behaviors even though you know better, and as a result create more stress—which in turn you try to manage with more old, defensive, self-destructive behaviors, which creates more stress, and so on.

The Doom Loop looks like this:

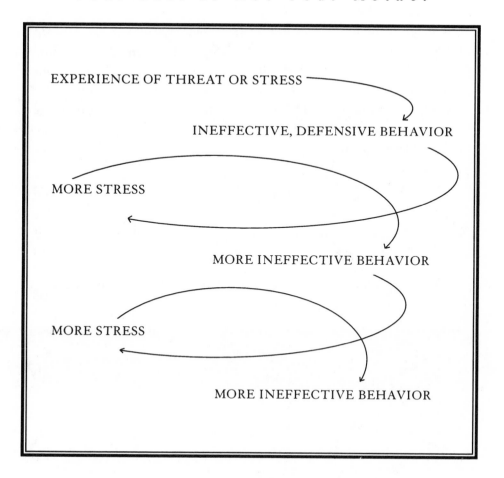

EXPERIENCE OF THREAT OR STRESS

INEFFECTIVE, DEFENSIVE BEHAVIOR

MORE STRESS

MORE INEFFECTIVE BEHAVIOR

MORE STRESS

MORE INEFFECTIVE BEHAVIOR

My seminar participants often say things like, "I know what I'm do-ing is hurting me, but I can't seem to stop." We learned these old pat-terns early in life and practiced them for many years, so changing them requires some attention. If you find yourself involved in The Doom Loop, don't beat yourself up. Just notice what is happening and disen-gage yourself from the situation as best you can. If you can't detach emo-tionally and change your behavior, you may have to leave the situation physically—at least until you become more objective and can choose a more productive path of action.

It often takes a major problem—the threat of being fired, an illness, or losing a promotion—before people step out of The Doom Loop. Other people can stop just by using such simple techniques as visual re-minders. I often suggest to my clients that they write notes to themselves about the benefits of letting go of family patterns, and to keep those pieces of paper above their desks or in their purses or pockets. Others wear a ring turned around or set their watch alarms at certain intervals as reminders. One executive put a small duck decal on her computer to remind herself to stop a pattern of chronic complaining.

These are some questions to help you recognize when you are caught in The Doom Loop:

- Are your personal relationships or physical health being affected by difficulties with people at work?

- Do you worry about what people at work think of you or feel anxious that they think you're incompetent?

- Do you avoid certain people, even though you have to interact with them in order to do your job?

- Do you commit yourself to unreasonable deadlines to keep the peace or avoid problems?

- Do you feel your self-confidence is decreasing, but hide behind a mask of activity and hard work?

- Do you have a history of frequent job changes?

- Has anyone at work ever told you that you seem overwhelmed, anxious, or upset a lot of the time?

If you answer yes to several of these questions, you may be caught in The Doom Loop. Getting unstuck takes some determination, but you'll see almost immediate results in your relationships with bosses, coworkers, and staff.

The Doom Loop is most often associated with three major behavior patterns at work:

- Denial, avoidance, and self-deception

- Rigid and highly competitive covert power games

- Corporate mixed messages that both espouse and punish open and honest communication

▣ POWER TOOL #4: DISENGAGE FROM UNHEALTHY EMOTIONAL TRIANGLES

As we have seen, emotional triangles occur when two people team up against a third. The goal is always to relieve stress in some way—by diminishing the tension between the two partners or by propping up someone's ego—but the result is usually to create even more stress.

The three steps to disengaging from unhealthy emotional triangles are:

1. Recognize the warning signs so that you can tell when an emotional triangle is forming and sidestep it. Start by noticing both internal and external clues. Do you have any physical sensations when someone starts telling you about his or her problems with another person? Do you feel tightness in your chest or stomach? Do you hold your breath or feel agitated?

What are your mental and emotional reactions? Do you get overly concerned about the other person's well-being or feel pressure to take care of him or her? Do you obsess about emotional issues between people at work rather than focusing on your own issues?

Under what conditions do you tend to be lured into triangles? Are you the one who pulls in a third person when you feel friction with someone? Or are you often the third person whom people draw in?

If someone says to you, "Don't tell anyone what I'm about to tell you," watch out! Secrets about people always create triangles. If you keep someone's secret, you've automatically taken that person's side against the person from whom you must keep the secret. To avoid becoming a conspirator, ask the person what he or she expects you to do with the secret. Better yet, tell the person you don't want to be involved in secrets at all.

Answer these questions to see the triangles you're most likely to create:

* When you form a triangle, who is usually involved?

* What do you do to get someone on your side?

* What do you hope will happen by forming a triangle?

If you find yourself being pulled into triangles even though you see them coming, you can use this next technique.

2. Deflect the stress that other people are trying to unload on you by pulling you into the triangle. To do this, acknowledge their discomfort without rescuing them from their feelings. Let people know that you understand and appreciate what they are feeling, and that you empathize with the stressful situation, but that you will not take sides.

It often helps to restate what they have said in your own words so that they know you were listening. An example:

SPEAKER: "Wes always singles me out when things go wrong. He just doesn't like anybody, does he?"
RESPONSE: "I don't know. You seem to feel ignored and upset by his behavior."

To keep from intervening on someone's behalf, ask specifically what he or she expects of you. Find out what you can do that he or she can't.

SPEAKER: "I can't get past Dave. He seems to block me every time. Will you talk to him for me?"
RESPONSE: "I hear that you feel Dave blocks you. I'm not sure exactly what you want me to do. What do you think I can accomplish that you can't?"

Also ask if the third party knows what is being discussed and make a policy of not talking about people unless they are present. If your supervisor tries to pull you into a conversation about another employee's performance, say either that you don't want to get caught in the middle or that you are uncomfortable talking about the other person when he or she isn't present. Be careful how you do this. Rather than appearing to criticize your supervisor for gossiping, make talking about the other employee *your* problem. Otherwise, the supervisor may get upset or feel guilty—and take it out on you.

It is not unusual for a boss to seek information about the performance of an employee from other employees. The problem arises from the fact that the employee in question probably doesn't know what's going on. *Remember: the stressful patterns of the emotional system live on secrecy and avoidance*. If your boss wants to involve you in a secret alliance, then see it for what it is: his or her own covert pattern to avoid dealing openly with the situation with that employee. The bottom line is: Except in situations when people's physical safety is at stake, it is neither appropriate nor healthy for you to be consulted about the performance of others in secrecy.

There are two similar ways you can get pulled into a secret alliance with your boss. The first involves a statement followed by a question.

> SPEAKER: "I don't think Ralph is pulling his weight, do you?"
> (Your boss is at least letting you know what he thinks.)
> RESPONSE: "Have you told him you're concerned? I'm not comfortable talking about him if he doesn't know you're concerned. If he says anything to me, then I don't want to have to pretend you didn't talk to me."

The second involves only a question.

> SPEAKER: "Do you think Ralph is pulling his weight?" (If your boss asks you any kind of a question about the performance of another employee in this format, watch out! You're probably being tested to see if you agree with the opinion that your boss has already formed but won't tell you. Whether you agree or disagree, you're still caught in the triangle. Turn it back to your boss immediately.)
> RESPONSE: "I don't know. Have you talked to Ralph? I'd feel better talking about Ralph if he were here.

3. Extract yourself from triangles in which you get caught. The minute you stop acting as the bank where people can deposit tension in their relationships with others, you are out of the triangle.

Encourage people to talk to the person with whom they have a problem rather than to you. Don't let George release his anger at Emily by using you as a listening post; tell him to speak directly to her. Make your position clear. Waffling and placating can get you into trouble, because people hear what they want to hear and interpret unclear statements to suit their own purposes.

WAFFLING: "George, I have to go now. Why don't you mention this to Emily at some point?"

BEING CLEAR: "George, I'm uncomfortable talking about Emily with you and don't want to do it anymore. I suggest you handle the problem directly with her or with the Personnel Department."

At times, people will genuinely ask you for help in dealing with another person. These genuine requests are marked by four distinct factors:

• The person asking for help talks about himself using No-Fault Thinking and "I"-Centered Communication (see Power Tool #5).

• The discussion is about specific behaviors, not personalities.

• You probably aren't familiar with the person in question.

• You don't feel caught in a secret or someone's covert power game.

We all get involved in emotional triangles from time to time because they are such a strong dynamic in families. Learning to disengage from them—and eventually to avoid them entirely—is one of the most important skills you will master.

This process of disengagement will prove most beneficial in dealing with the following patterns of behavior:

• The roles of Victim, Rescuer or Persecutor

• Covert power games, particularly complaining, criticizing, and blaming

• Covert rules and mixed messages about secrecy.

▣ POWER TOOL #5: USE "I"-CENTERED COMMUNICATION

One of the fastest ways to improve your relationships at work is to make statements that begin with "I" rather than with "You"—especially if your message may make someone uncomfortable or if the other person may interpret it as a challenge to his or her competence, authority, or integrity.

Notice the difference between these two statements:

"YOU"-CENTERED COMMUNICATION: "You're making me late with my reports."

"I"-CENTERED COMMUNICATION: "When I don't get the reports from you on time, my schedule backs up and I have to delay other work. Is there a way to get them to me on time?"

The first statement is an accusation; the second is a request for help and support. Most people would rather hear the second statement. They feel less threatened when you are talking about yourself than they do when you are talking about their performance—and when they feel less threatened, they are less likely to slip into old family defenses.

Using "I"-statements is particularly important in times of stress, when you may be tempted to blame others for problems. *Speaking* about the problem as if it were your own responsibility may help you *think* that way as well. Keep the focus on yourself—especially when you suspect that a problem may actually be someone else's responsibility. This helps others to stay open to you and makes for effective problem solving.

"I want . . ." statements are a good way to communicate your desires to others:

- "I want to understand the new policies, so could you review the major changes?" (*Not:* "You need to explain the new policies more clearly.")

- "I don't want to be misunderstood, so I'm going to explain my position." (*Not:* "You're not hearing me. Stop talking and listen.")

- "I want to be more open with you, but I'm not sure of what you'll think of me if I tell you my concerns about what happened in the meeting." (*Not:* "You're so judgmental that no one dares talk to you about problems.")

"I feel . . ." statements are a good way to tell others you're upset without blaming them. Be specific about what they did that triggered your reaction so that they can change their behavior if they choose to do so.

- "When your report is late, I feel upset." (*Not:* "You make me furious when your work is late.")

- "I felt irritated by what you said about my work in the meeting. I want to discuss it." (*Not:* "You were criticizing me.")

- "I feel left out of the project when you don't send me memos about changes in the schedule." (*Not:* "You're cutting me out of the loop and making me do bad work.")

- "When you take phone calls while I'm meeting with you, I feel unimportant and like I'm intruding." (*Not:* "You're power-tripping me and I hate it.")

Reflective "I"-statements let you clarify what has been said to or about you. Restate the situation to make sure that you and the other person have the same understanding of what is going on.

- "Do I hear you saying that I caused you to be late with your work by not completing the report on time?"

- "Am I right that you don't want to talk about this project right now?"

- "Are you saying that you want me to work overtime?"

A caution: *True "I"-statements do not contain hidden "You"-statements.* Sal told his administrative assistant, Anne, "I feel like you aren't telling me everything that's going on in your area." Anne accused him of not trusting her, a reaction Sal had not anticipated, since he'd been so careful to say "I." When he thought about it later, he realized he'd actually made a "You"-statement and stuck "I feel . . ." at the beginning of the sentence. If the message had been a true "I"-statement, he might have said, "I feel frustrated and uncomfortable when I don't know what projects you're working on."

Statements that begin, "I feel that you . . ." or "I think that you . . ." often contain hidden "You"-statements and almost always elicit a defensive reaction.

What do you do when an "I"-statement backfires? Occasionally, you'll run across someone who is uncomfortable with "I"-messages. When you speak about your own experience, your own thoughts, and your own feelings, you make powerful statements about yourself. Some people aren't used to this direct form of communication and find it upsetting because they are accustomed to more covert communications. The antidote is to acknowledge what you see happening ("I sense that you are upset—are you?") and what you want to have happen ("I want to resolve our differences").

◘ Using "I"-statements keeps the focus on your own thoughts, feelings, and behavior. You become more aware of how others influence you, minimize your reactions to them, and can make better choices about what and how to communicate.

The behaviors that can be most effectively changed through "I"-Centered Communication include:

• Denial and avoidance

• The roles of Hero, Caretaker, Mascot, and Scapegoat

• Covert power games.

◘ POWER TOOL #6: CLARIFY MIXED MESSAGES—YOUR OWN AND OTHER PEOPLE'S

Clarifying confused communications from others brings their real meaning to the surface so that you don't have to operate in two realities: what they say and what they mean. Clarifying your own mixed messages makes you a more effective communicator and keeps your connections with others from being clouded by uncertainty and unconscious resentment.

Use these techniques to help clarify mixed messages you receive from others:

• *Acknowledge both what is said and what you sense the speaker really means.* It might sound like this: "I hear that you want me to take the trip to Denver, but I am confused because you don't sound enthusiastic. I'd like to talk about it." Essentially, you are stating the two realities side by side and asking the other person either to choose one or to acknowledge that both are true.

• *Ask people to clarify mixed messages in private* so that they don't feel threatened or embarrassed by being confronted in public.

• *Choose a time when you can finish the discussion.* Don't try to have these talks on the run or at times when you're likely to be interrupted. If you leave part of the discussion hanging, even temporarily, it may become distorted, or the other person may start feeling threatened or defensive.

• *Remember that most people don't know they're giving mixed messages.* Blaming people for giving mixed messages will only make them more defensive. They aren't necessarily doing it to be difficult; mixed messages are simply a habit with most of us, defense mechanisms that have become a part of our culture. Instead, focus on yourself and the conflicts you feel. Use "I"-messages to describe your feelings, observations, or sense of what is going on. Say things like, "When you tell me I'm important to the project but don't inform me about meetings, I feel confused. Do you really want me to participate?"

• *Practice not reacting to mixed messages at work as you did to mixed messages in your family.* The most common reactions to mixed messages are anger and sullen withdrawal, neither of which is an effective response at work. Learn to recognize the specific reactions you learned in your family so that you can step back and avoid escalating the situation.

To avoid giving mixed messages yourself, use these two techniques:

• *Be direct.* Say what you mean, even if the information is unpleasant or may upset people.

- *Become familiar with the mixed messages in your family,* and remember that these are the ones you're most likely to deliver.

Clarifying mixed messages doesn't mean you'll always get the answers you want, but you'll at least know where you stand and what you can expect. As with most of the Power Tools discussed in this chapter, you may get a strong defensive reaction to identifying a mixed message with someone, even if you are completely nonblaming and "I"-centered in your communication. Remember, your strength lies not in behaving according to an old pattern but in using the tools you have to exercise choice about your response.

Clarifying mixed messages is instrumental in identifying and changing the following patterns:

- Covert rules or norms that govern how conflicts and differences are resolved

- Covert power games, particularly sarcasm, ridicule, and indirect criticism and innuendo.

▣   POWER TOOL #7: DEVELOP CONFLICT-RESOLUTION SKILLS

When everybody's family patterns start ricocheting around the office, conflicts inevitably arise. While this book shows you how to resolve those conflicts at their source—habitual family-patterned reactions to stress—it is sometimes necessary to learn how to treat the symptoms— two people at each other's throats, literally or figuratively.

Many books, tapes, and seminars offer help with conflict-resolution skills, and you can use these general guidelines as you start to apply them:

- *Be open to new information.* Many conflicts begin when people react defensively to information that they feel threatens their security, their self-esteem, or their desires to feel included, competent, and liked. Listen openly and respectfully to new input so that it doesn't throw you back into old family patterns.

- *Handle the underlying emotional issue first—your own and the other person's—and the rest of the conflict will be much easier to resolve.* Most conflicts have two parts: the surface issue and the underlying emotional issue. The order in which the parts are addressed may determine whether the conflict is successfully resolved. For example, when the company moved to a new suite, Collin was angry that Irv, whose position in the company was exactly parallel to his, appeared to be getting the larger, more attractive office. In fact, Collin didn't really care what his office looked like—but he was afraid the office assignment meant that Irv had more prestige in the company, that people thought he was more competent, or even that Irv was about to be promoted over him. The surface issue was the office assignment; the underlying emotional issue was that Collin's competence felt threatened.

  If Collin doesn't handle the emotional part first, it may become extremely difficult to resolve the conflict. He may spend days talking about offices, only to have another conflict about desk chairs if his underlying emotional issue isn't identified.

  Collin's fears may be justified. Perhaps Irv is going to be promoted over him. However, Collin won't be able to deal effectively with Irv or his company's decision about Irv's promotion when he's caught up in an emotionally reactive pattern.

  In any conflict, always deal with your emotions first by taking time to let them cool down. The same holds true for dealing with someone caught in the grip of anger or defensiveness. It will be almost impossible to speak calmly or be heard until the feelings have been acknowledged or at least subsided. It can be beneficial to think of your own or anyone else's anger or defensiveness as a reaction to a threat to the emotional desires for inclusion, control, or openness.

- *Communicate respectfully and directly.* Communicate with others as you would like them to communicate with you. Many conflicts can be resolved or avoided altogether if you maintain an attitude of honesty and respect.

Developing your conflict resolution skills will help you to feel competent to handle the many problems that spring up in relationships, particularly:

- Covert power plays
- The Persecutor role
- Covert rules that inhibit open discussion of differences.

▣ POWER TOOL #8: AVOID POWER PLAYS: DON'T TRY TO CHANGE OTHERS OR CONTROL THEIR BEHAVIOR

As we saw in Chapter 8, all covert power games are attempts to control others' behavior—and the stress that their behavior produces in us. Avoiding these defensive tactics eliminates a huge group of family patterns from the office environment.

We resort to these power plays because we don't know what else to do. Most of us never learned in our families to ask for recognition, confront people who were verbally abusive, or communicate our desires and experiences in direct and straightforward ways.

The four keys to avoiding covert power games are:

- *Recognize the Six Signs of Defensiveness* listed in Chapter 8, because we're most likely to fall into power games when we feel defensive or threatened. Those signs are: high emotional charge, rigid thinking, teaching and preaching, blaming or ridiculing, pretending to feel confused or stupid, and cynicism or sarcasm.

- *Remember that covert power games never really work.* You can't change or manipulate others' behavior in the long term. You may push them into certain behaviors temporarily, but the results won't last and you probably won't feel very good about yourself. Power games are a waste of time because they sap energy, diminish effectiveness and self-esteem, and produce results that are at best both temporary and demeaning.

- *Explore how covert power games were played in your family, and what instinctive reactions you learned to them.* The games that you and your family played are the ones most likely to show up at your office.

- *Practice, practice, practice.* Most people don't stop playing covert power games overnight. These games can be subtle, and we've been playing them for so long that sometimes we don't even know that we're doing it. Don't beat yourself up if you fall into them occasionally. Just notice that you've done so, pick yourself up, and try again. Each time you see that you've avoided slipping into a power play, give yourself a pat on the back.

By working on avoiding power games you'll also be focusing your efforts to change other patterns in your life or work environment, including:

- Roles you play

- Rules that foster cutthroat competition

- Mixed messages regarding office politics.

▣ POWER TOOL #9: SWITCH YOUR FOCUS FROM PROBLEMS TO SOLUTIONS—AND LOOK FOR REAL SOLUTIONS, NOT BANDAGES

Focusing on problems keeps you stuck in a downward spiral of negative thinking—yet many people find this habit hard to break because it protects them from a potentially more difficult and uncomfortable task: finding solutions.

In family systems therapy, we've found that finding real solutions means dealing with core personal issues, and that may involve facing uncomfortable truths about yourself and the emotional dynamics you learned as a child. You may see, for instance, that the real problem in your relationship with your boss is that you've been expecting him to behave as the Tyrant your father was and reacting to him as the Victim you were in your family. When you recognize that dynamic, you may have to do something about it. Changing lifelong emotional habits is usually much more uncomfortable than focusing on the problem by complaining about your boss, or than applying the bandage of taking a vacation or trying to get transferred.

You can practice focusing on solutions by asking yourself whenever you feel pressure to solve a relationship problem: How might this situation be the result of an emotional dynamic that I brought to work?

Focusing on problems is often an attempt to eliminate stress without facing difficult issues or making any real changes. Part 3 shows you how to find effective solutions.

Changing your focus from problem finding to solution seeking will bring you additional benefits by helping you to resolve these patterns:

- The Victim, Rescuer, Caretaker, and Rebel roles

- Covert power games

- Internalized rules that inhibit you from expressing your creativity or abilities for fear of failure.

▣ POWER TOOL #10: SHIFT FROM OUTER- TO INNER-CENTERED REALITY

Outer-centered reality means seeing yourself as you think others see you rather than how you see yourself, and believing that other people and external circumstances are responsible for what happens in your life. It usually means looking over your shoulder to see what others think of you, reacting defensively to what they say and do, figuring out what they have done to cause your problems, and trying to change their behavior.

Outer-centered reality almost always triggers old defensive tactics because your attention is *out there*. You rely on others for validation and blame them when something goes wrong.

Inner-centered reality puts the focus on you. What's important is what *you* think about yourself, and how you handle the people and events around you. You assume responsibility for your own thoughts and feelings and take control of your life. You own your problems and understand that only you can solve them.

There are some genuine problems *out there*—gender and cultural bias, abuses of power within a hierarchical system, disrespectful and dishonest management practices—but you only have dominion over your own reactions, thoughts, feelings, and behaviors. You can control how you respond to situations outside yourself, and that control comes from developing an inner-centered reality.

The shift to an inner-centered reality is, again, not something you should expect to happen by tomorrow afternoon. It takes practice and patience, but it will give you authority in situations you never dreamed you could master.

It will also enable you to identify and resolve ineffective behavior patterns in other areas of your life:

- The Superachiever or Hero role

- Self-deception

- Covert power games

- Rules that have carried over from your family to your workplace.

□ POWER TOOL #11: KEEP YOUR
  ROLES, RULES, AND WAYS OF
  RELATING FLEXIBLE

When you always play the same part in the office drama—Superachiever, Victim, "Bad" Child, Martyr, Rebel, Rescuer, etc.—you lose your ability to roll with the punches, deal with new situations, and solve problems. Life becomes static, because you have only a limited number of responses to any situation.

The roles, rules, and ways of relating that are most likely to become rigid are the ones you learned in your family. When you can avoid slipping automatically into these dynamics, you're better able to adopt whatever roles or responses are appropriate to the situation, and to adjust to changing circumstances without going crazy.

Being flexible doesn't mean you're wishy-washy; it is actually a sign of strength and conviction. It means you are a big enough person to be resilient and open to new information.

When you feel stuck and powerless, when problems at work don't seem to get solved, or when you catch yourself defending your behavior by telling someone, "That's just the way I am," stop and check to see if you've fallen into a role, rule, or way of relating that occurred in your family. Do the exercises in Part 3 to see what you can change about that behavior and how best to go about it.

The higher your degree of flexibility, the more open you will be to receiving new information without getting lost in defensive emotions. This will help you deal with and change any behaviors you have learned and developed that are no longer useful to you, particularly:

• Rigid power games

• Repetitive roles that are often Doom Loops such as Scapegoat/Rebel, Rescuer/Caretaker, and Clown/Mascot.

▣ POWER TOOL #12: CLAIM HIGH SELF-ESTEEM

High self-esteem has nothing to do with having your name or title on a door, earning the corner office, being technically or intellectually proficient, or becoming the salesperson of the year. It has to do with how you think and feel about yourself and how well you relate to others.

People with high self-esteem don't have to change or avoid others in order to feel good about themselves. They are confident about who they are and secure in their ability to respond effectively under stress. They know the power of staying in touch with their thoughts and feelings without reacting.

People with low self-esteem are more likely to react defensively. They tend to worry about what others think of them and waste valuable time and energy defending themselves against what they perceive as threats. Their ability to deal with conflicts or resolve differences is marginal because these activities feel too threatening.

The next time you let someone's behavior upset you, ask yourself what that person did to earn so much control over your thoughts and feelings. Remember that no one should have as much dominion in your life as you do, and that part of high self-esteem is the power to choose how you respond to people and events.

Claiming high self-esteem is a subtle, internal matter. You can read all the books, follow all the how-to steps, and not really feel that inner sense of self-worth. That's why I use the word *claim*. Self-esteem is a matter of experiencing yourself as a valuable individual and recognizing that you have a right to think of yourself that way. It's yours whenever you're ready to reach out and claim it.

High self-esteem and rigid patterns of stressful behavior are practically opposites. As you work on changing the patterns that keep you stuck and reactive, your self-esteem will increase. Specifically, high self-esteem will enable you to alter:

- Any ineffective ways of relating

- Internal beliefs/rules that promote a sense of inadequacy or unworthiness.

▣ POWER TOOL #13: EMPOWER YOURSELF

Personal growth is a process of transforming old habits, perceptions, and emotional dynamics into new and more productive ones. When you let go of old patterns, you do two extremely powerful things:

- *You stop trying to do the impossible*—control or change others.

- *You concentrate on the possible*—developing your own way of thriving in relationships at work.

The dictionary defines *empower* as "to authorize, to enable, to permit." To empower yourself means to authorize yourself to take charge of your reactions and develop new ways of relating to others that affirm yourself and support them. You assume responsibility for making changes in yourself and for enjoying the positive results. You become the captain of your own ship, instead of being buffeted by the moods and behaviors of others.

When you practice using the techniques in this chapter on a daily basis, you embark on a journey of empowerment. You take control of your life and relationships at work and start discovering strengths and abilities within yourself that you may never have noticed before.

In Part 3, you will start exploring what specific changes you want to make. You will learn tools and strategies for making those changes within a system that resists change, and you will set specific goals. As you move forward, use the skills you've learned in this chapter to make those changes more quickly and easily.

MAKING CHANGES: SIX ACTION STEPS

I n Part 1, you looked at how family patterns work and why they show up at the office in times of stress. In Part 2, you explored the particular defensive emotional patterns that you learned in your own family.

Part 3 is about making changes in those attitudes and behaviors so that your work relationships become healthier, more supportive, and more productive. You will identify what specific changes you want to make, assess the risks involved, and decide how best to go about them.

The first six chapters in Part 3 cover the Six Action Steps for Change:

SIX ACTION STEPS FOR CHANGE

1. *Map the emotional dynamics in your office.*
2. *Map the emotional dynamics in your family.*
3. *Assess the risks of possible changes.*
4. *Choose what you want to do differently.*
5. *Plan for resistance.*
6. *Make the change and assess the results.*

The final chapter describes the unexpected benefits of transforming your work relationships by learning to recognize family patterns and changing your behavior.

Some of the exercises in Part 3 may seem unnecessary, and others may make you uncomfortable. I strongly recommend that you do them all, especially if they seem unnecessary or make you uncomfortable, since these reactions are often clues you may be avoiding something. They will provide you with invaluable information that generates specific solutions for your individual situation. Initiating changes before you have gathered and assessed all this information can jeopardize your relationships at work and even your job.

Do these exercises at your own pace, without rushing. Think of them as an investment in yourself, a way to experience more satisfaction and more success at work—and eventually in every area of your life.

You'll be following the same process that Alice, one of my clients, used to change a destructive Doom Loop that was damaging to her physical health and hurting her career. Her experience will illustrate how these Six Action Steps for Change can create a genuine sense of empowerment for you.

11

Step #1: Map the Emotional Dynamics in Your Office

W hen things start to fall apart at work, it can be difficult to figure out what's really going on. Relationships feel disjointed, uncomfortable, even hostile. Tasks don't flow smoothly. Nobody seems to be experiencing "wins." Yet in the midst of all the chaos, it's hard to see exactly what went wrong and what's at the core of the problem—unless you already know something about how your office's emotional dynamics work.

In this chapter, we'll lay out the dynamics in your workplace piece by piece so that you understand exactly how the relationships are wired up, how invisible realities affect everyday situations, where problems are most likely to surface, and what impact all of this has on you.

You will map both the official and the underground relationships, the stated and unstated rules, the emotional realities behind the corporate facade, the power games and office politics. You'll see just where you fit into the picture, and that knowledge will give you power.

We will use my client Alice's work as an example throughout this section, so let's look at her situation.

■ ALICE'S OFFICE

Alice worked as director of publications in the Public Information Department of a nonprofit safety council that provided public-safety education and services in a ten-state region. She learned how quickly she could slip into family patterns when she spent three months working on a huge promotional project with her lackluster colleagues, Ed and Connie.

Alice got her work done more quickly than the others and began helping Ed and Connie, but with three weeks to go, the project started falling behind. Their boss Rick called Alice in and said the organization's president, Earl, was pressuring him for interim results. Rick wanted Alice to put pressure on Ed and Connie and, "You know, do your miracle-worker thing."

Rick had a habit of coercing Alice into squeezing Ed and Connie for results, even though Ed and Connie were on the same level as Alice, and Alice had no real authority over them. She didn't like being manipulated into doing his job as well as her own and knew that Rick was just afraid Ed and Connie wouldn't like him if he got tough—but there was something in her that couldn't stand to see the project fail and was willing to do anything to save it.

She also knew that Rick was terrified of his boss, Earl, a large, jovial man who had been a colonel in the army. Alice had mixed feelings about Earl. She sensed he was ineffective, but she also wanted his approval and acknowledgment for all her miracles and achievements—things for which she suspected Rick was taking credit.

She felt surrounded by dolts who either didn't know how to get things done or didn't care. The organization's primary unwritten rule was: We are a nonprofit and don't have to swim with the sharks. We're here to take it easy, or because we couldn't make it elsewhere. Nobody puts much pressure on anybody else to achieve. Alice was beginning to suspect that the higher people rose in the organization, the more that rule applied.

Before Alice could bully Ed and Connie into shape, Earl called them all in and asked how the work was going. "Great!" Ed beamed. "We should be finished early." Connie gave Ed a fishy look, then stared at the carpet. Alice was so angry she could feel her heart pounding in her chest. When they left the meeting, she barked at Ed and Connie, "I want to see you guys in my office right away."

She sat them down, unilaterally appointed herself director of the project, broke the work down into small segments, and assigned deadlines for each task as if Ed and Connie were inept children. Connie burst into tears and said she couldn't work like that. Ed charged to Connie's defense and told Alice she was just making matters worse with her "bossy, heavy-handed attitude." Alice knew her management style left something to be desired and apologized halfheartedly. Ed was resentful and Connie withdrawn, but they both realized that Alice's plan was the only way to get the project done.

Alice felt as if she needed four hands: two to keep Ed and Connie in line, one to placate Rick, and another to suggest somehow to Earl that she was the one doing all the work. She tried to relieve some of the stress by gossiping with her secretary Marcia, whose loyalty was absolute.

Marcia was a quiet woman who often disappeared into the woodwork when people around her got upset but did all her work perfectly and ahead of schedule. She was appalled that anyone would challenge her wonderful boss, Alice, and immediately formed an alliance with Ed's secretary, Sarah, against him. Sarah was disgusted with Ed because he was incompetent and had called her "Honey" and asked her to get coffee on her first day at work. Now she had a perfect opportunity to strike back at him and make him look bad. Unfortunately, undercutting his work also hurt Alice because Ed was on her team.

The project got finished late the night before it was due, but Connie felt used, Ed was furious, and Alice was filled with guilt for her cutthroat tactics and resentment for having to do everything. Nobody enjoyed the project or felt much satisfaction from it. Alice, Ed, and Connie all had bad feelings about one another, their work, and the organization.

Alice came to me because she knew her bullying tactics weren't working and she felt out of control. She wasn't a monster, she told me, and wanted to relate to people with more mutual respect, trust, and warmth.

I suggested she start by completing the exercises in this chapter. We literally mapped the emotional environment at the safety council so that she could see clearly, from a bird's-eye view, what was happening. Before she could consider changes, she needed to know exactly what dynamics were already in place. Use Alice's answers as examples as you map the emotional environment in your organization.

▣ YOUR VISIBLE ORGANIZATIONAL CHART

Draw an organizational chart of your work group. This is the stated, visible hierarchy that shows who has authority over whom, and reflects how your organization looks to outsiders. The chart should include no more than ten individuals who directly affect your job or with whom you work. Alice's organizational chart looked like this:

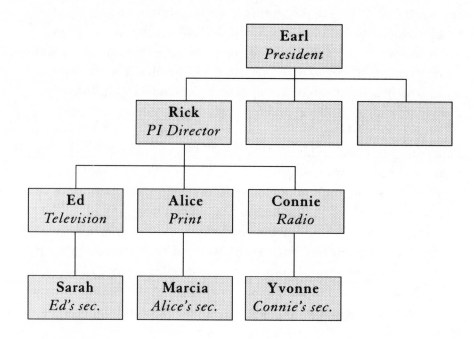

▣ YOUR INVISIBLE ORGANIZATIONAL CHART

Now create an Invisible Organizational Chart. This will show how people *really* relate to one another—what goes on behind the facade of the organizational chart. It will bring hidden emotional dynamics to the surface and demystify the relationships in your office. You will add to this chart in subsequent exercises, and a clear picture of what's actually going on among the people with whom you work will emerge.

Instructions: Place the names of everyone in your work group around the perimeter of a circle, with each person's job title next to his or her name. Draw rectangles around the names and titles of men, and circles around the names and titles of women.

Alice's chart looked like this:

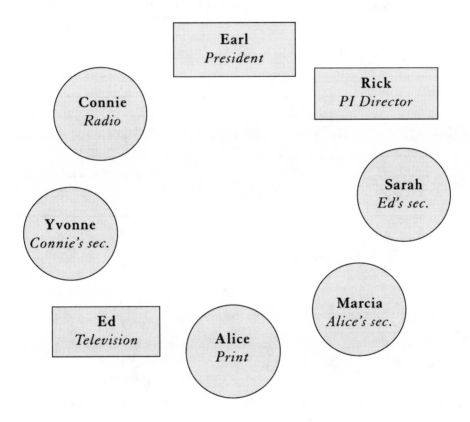

Roles in Your Workplace

Roles are the parts we learned to play in our families whenever we felt threatened and didn't know what else to do. Some of the roles we've discussed are Superachiever, Victim, Rescuer, Martyr, "Bad" Child,

Quiet "Good" Child, and Clown. You may discover others that are unique to your work group as you start looking at what role each person plays. Keep in mind that a role is basically a label for an overriding behavior pattern.

Instructions: List the role or roles played by each person you included on your Invisible Organizational Chart. Enter each person's roles next to his or her name on the chart. If you have trouble identifying people's roles, picture yourself at a tension-filled meeting with everyone you listed on the emotional map of your workplace. How is each person acting? Remember, people may play more than one role.

NAME AND POSITION   ROLE(S)

_____   _____
_____   _____
_____   _____
_____   _____
_____   _____
_____   _____
_____   _____
_____   _____

Alice's list looked like this:

NAME AND POSITION	ROLE(S)
Earl—President	Persecutor
	Clown and Jokester
Rick—Director of Public Information	People Pleaser
	Victim (of Earl)
Ed—Television specialist	Rescuer (of Connie)
	Rebel (against Alice)
	Persecutor (of Alice)
Connie—Radio specialist	Victim
Marcia—Alice's secretary	Lost Child
	Rescuer (of Alice)
Sarah—Ed's secretary	Rebel
Yvonne—Connie's secretary	Caretaker/Rescuer

Your Personal Roles

The most important part of this exercise may be examining what role or roles you play at work. Think about the "parts" for which you reach instinctively when you feel stressed. If you have trouble seeing which role or roles you play, reread Chapters 4–6.

Alice saw that her most common role was what she perceived as Superachiever, and Ed and Connie perceived as Persecutor—but she could also slip into being the Victim of Earl's indifference, of Rick's manipulation, or of Ed's power games. Alice was also a Rescuer to Rick because she kept Earl off his back by producing results. None of these complex and convoluted relationships was acknowledged on the organizational chart. Even Alice hadn't been aware of them all until she started writing them down.

Instructions: Make a list of the roles you play at work, and the people with whom you play them. Add your roles to your Invisible Organizational Chart.

THE ROLES I PLAY ARE: I PLAY THESE ROLES WITH:

_____   _____

_____   _____

_____   _____

_____   _____

_____   _____

Here are Alice's answers:

THE ROLES I PLAY ARE:	I PLAY THESE ROLES WITH:
Superachiever	Myself, Marcia, Rick
Persecutor	Ed, Connie
Victim	Earl, Rick, Ed
Rescuer	Rick

When Alice had finished this exercise, her Invisible Organizational Chart looked like this:

ROLES: Persecutor, Clown

Earl
President

ROLES: Victim

Connie
Radio

ROLES: People Pleaser, Victim

Rick
PI Director

Yvonne
Connie's sec.

Sarah
Ed's sec.

ROLES: Caretaker, Rescuer

ROLES: Rebel

Ed
Television

ROLES: Rescuer, Rebel, Persecutor

Marcia
Alice's sec.

ROLES: Lost Child, Rescuer

Alice
Print

ROLES: Super Achiever, Persecutor, Rescuer

Ways of Relating in Your Workplace

We've seen that some of the ineffective, unhealthy ways of relating that people learn in their families and bring to work under stress are: denial, avoidance, withdrawal, attacking, manipulation, smothering, bullying, emotional bribery, control, placating, blaming, playing Victim, shaming, criticizing, the silent treatment, intimidation, gossiping, rescuing, domination, patronizing or condescension, threats, and verbal or physical abuse.

Instructions: List the primary ways of relating that each person in your office uses during stressful times and interactions: conflicts, disagreements, deadline crises, and so on. Add this information to your Invisible Organizational Chart.

PERSON   WAYS OF RELATING

_____

_____

_____

_____

_____

Here is Alice's list:

PERSON	WAYS OF RELATING
Earl	Smothering, controlling, intimidation
Rick	People pleasing, emotional bribery
Ed	Attacking, rescuing
Connie	Playing Victim, silent treatment
Marcia	Withdrawing, gossiping
Sarah	Rebelling, attacking
Yvonne	Rescuing

Your Personal Ways of Relating

We all have certain ways of relating that we use more than others when we feel stressed or threatened.

Instructions: Make a list of the ways in which you relate under stress, and the people with whom you relate this way. Add these to your Invisible Organizational Chart.

MY WAYS OF RELATING   TO:

_____   _____
_____   _____
_____   _____
_____   _____
_____   _____

This is Alice's list:

MY WAYS OF RELATING   TO:
Bullying, threats, intimidation   Ed, Connie
Placating, rescuing   Rick
Gossiping, rescuing   Marcia

This is how Alice's chart looked when she had done the exercises on invisible roles, rules, and ways of relating:

ROLES: Persecutor, Clown
WAYS OF RELATING:
Smothering, controlling,
intimidating

Earl
President

ROLES: Victim
WAYS OF RELATING:
Guilt-tripping, silence

ROLES: People Pleaser,
Victim
WAYS OF RELATING:
Placating, emotional bribery

Connie
Radio

Rick
PI Director

Yvonne
Connie's sec.

Sarah
Ed's sec.

ROLES: Caretaker,
Rescuer
WAYS OF RELATING:
Rescuing

ROLES: Rebel
WAYS OF RELATING:
Attacking

Ed
Television

Marcia
Alice's sec.

ROLES: Rescuer, Rebel,
Persecutor
WAYS OF RELATING:
Attacking, rescuing

ROLES: Lost Child,
Rescuer
WAYS OF RELATING:
Gossiping, with-
drawing

Alice
Print

ROLES: Super Achiever, Persecutor,
Rescuer
WAYS OF RELATING: Threats, intimida-
tion, placating, rescuing, gossiping

Emotional Triangles in Your Workplace

These entanglements are almost always unproductive because they are based on competition, animosity, anxiety, and exclusion. Some common triangles in organizations are:

- Two employees vying for the boss's favor

- One employee rescuing or protecting another from an oppressive boss

- Two employees forming an alliance against the boss

- A manager aligning first with one employee, then with another, to encourage competition between them

- Two colleagues aligning against a third

- Two bosses using an employee as go-between.

Instructions: List the emotional triangles in which you are involved at work. After each person's name, write the role that he or she plays in the triangle. Draw each of these triangles on your Invisible Organizational Chart.

PERSON #1 (ROLE)	PERSON #2 (ROLE)	PERSON #3 (ROLE)
_____	_____	_____
_____	_____	_____
_____	_____	_____
_____	_____	_____
_____	_____	_____

Alice's office was filled with emotional triangles:

PERSON #1 (ROLE)	PERSON #2 (ROLE)	PERSON #3 (ROLE)
Alice (Persecutor)	Connie (Victim)	Ed (Rescuer)
Earl (Persecutor)	Rick (Victim)	Alice (Rescuer)
Ed (Persecutor)	Alice/Marcia (Victims)	Marcia/Sarah (Rescuers)

Alice's final Invisible Organizational Chart looked like this:

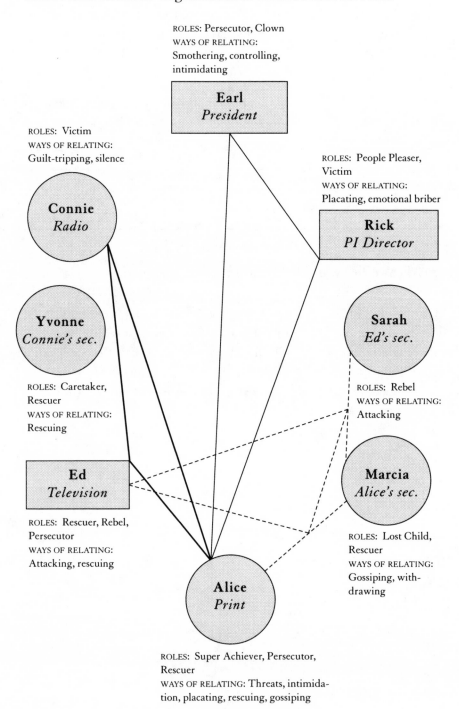

ROLES: Persecutor, Clown
WAYS OF RELATING:
Smothering, controlling,
intimidating

Earl
President

ROLES: Victim
WAYS OF RELATING:
Guilt-tripping, silence

ROLES: People Pleaser,
Victim
WAYS OF RELATING:
Placating, emotional briber

Connie
Radio

Rick
PI Director

Yvonne
Connie's sec.

Sarah
Ed's sec.

ROLES: Caretaker,
Rescuer
WAYS OF RELATING:
Rescuing

ROLES: Rebel
WAYS OF RELATING:
Attacking

Ed
Television

Marcia
Alice's sec.

ROLES: Rescuer, Rebel,
Persecutor
WAYS OF RELATING:
Attacking, rescuing

ROLES: Lost Child,
Rescuer
WAYS OF RELATING:
Gossiping, with-
drawing

Alice
Print

ROLES: Super Achiever, Persecutor,
Rescuer
WAYS OF RELATING: Threats, intimida-
tion, placating, rescuing, gossiping

▣ RULES IN YOUR WORKPLACE

What are the invisible rules that govern your workplace, the ones that nobody talks about but everybody follows? Consider the following questions:

- *What topics can't you bring up?* Many companies don't want people to talk about budgets, staff problems, or fudged expense accounts.

- *Do you have to hide any of your activities or beliefs?* One engineer told me he had to hide some research because he didn't want his boss to take the credit for it. Another client said she never talked politics with anyone at work, for fear of reprisals.

- *How do you and your coworkers deal with unpleasant feelings such as anger, sadness, hurt, shame, confusion. and fear?* What happens when you have and express these feelings?

- *Do you feel the need to avoid upsetting your supervisor with an unpleasant truth?* What if the way your boss acts is causing the company to lose customers or clients? Can you tell him or her? Can you tell anyone?

Instructions: Set aside the chart of the invisible organizational system. Make a separate list of the unwritten rules in your workplace.

- _____

- _____

- _____

- _____

- _____

- _____

These are some of the unwritten rules in Alice's company:

- Never disagree with Earl. Flatter his ego and make him feel competent, even though he isn't.

- If you have a problem, solve it yourself and don't bother your boss with it.

- Look busy, but don't produce much. We say we produce results, but we're here because we don't want to work hard. Never put pressure on another person to achieve, unless that person is a sucker and will make you look good.

Alice saw that she had followed all these rules except the last one, and that's what got her into trouble. She violated an ironclad, if secret, rule of the organization's corporate culture. Earl and Rick adhered to this rule. They went through the motions of looking busy and giving lip service to getting the project done—but neither of them was willing to step forward and crack the whip himself. They got Alice to step over that line and threaten everyone by suggesting that they did have to produce and might not be as safe and secure in their mediocrity as they had come to expect. Rick and Earl, once more, got to talk about excellence without demanding it of themselves or others—and Alice paid the price.

Your Personal Rules

Are there any rules that you impose on yourself without telling anyone? You may honestly believe that the company is imposing these rules on you, when, in fact, you've been living by them for some time—perhaps even since childhood. If you find some of the same difficult rules at each place you work, check to be sure they aren't self-imposed. Consider the following questions:

- *How do you feel about doing a good job when others appear to be slacking off? What words run through your mind?* Many people feel guilty about being effective at work for fear they will appear aloof or get excluded; others will increase their efforts to make up for the slack.

- *How tolerant are you of mixed messages because they come from authority?* One client adamantly refused to acknowledge that she was being sexually harassed because she had an internal rule that prohibited her from challenging authority figures.
- *When do you feel like you should do something or behave a certain way?* Often the "shoulds" in our lives are personal rules that we impose on ourselves.

Instructions: Make a list of your personal rules, ones you may have brought to work from your family.

- ____
- ____
- ____
- ____
- ____
- ____

Some of Alice's personal rules were:

- Be the best, no matter what it costs you.
- Take responsibility for other people getting their work done if it affects yours. You are in charge; make sure everything goes smoothly. If someone is in trouble, it's your job to help them.
- People will always fight you; it's your job to overcome adversity and get your work done anyway.
- Only perfection is acceptable; anything else gets you into trouble.

MIXED MESSAGES IN YOUR WORKPLACE

Mixed messages are so common that they may seem normal to you, but they create subtle, powerful stress. It's important to identify exactly what the mixed messages in your workplace are, so that you can start clarifying them one by one. The first sign of a mixed message is often confusion or a gut sense that something is off. Ask yourself when or around whom you feel confused at work.

Instructions: Make a list of the mixed messages in your workplace.

Mixed Messages in My Workplace:

+ _____

+ _____

+ _____

+ _____

+ _____

+ _____

Here is Alice's list:

Mixed Messages in My Workplace:

- They claim to hire competent people and demand excellence, but everybody slacks off.

- Earl is often on TV news talking about how deeply committed everyone here is to safety, but everybody here just wants to collect a paycheck and go home.

- The organization talks about teamwork, but everybody tries to get by doing as little as possible.

- Everybody is supposed to support one another in doing this great service to humankind, but you can't ever tell anyone you have a problem with your work. You have to hide mistakes or come up with your own solutions.

◩ NOW WHAT?

The exercises you've just completed should give you a clear picture of the emotional dynamics in your workplace and how people's hidden roles, rules, and ways of relating are often different from their stated, visible ones. You should also have some idea what part you play in these dynamics.

Alice found this part of her homework somewhat uncomfortable but extremely interesting. She could look back with twenty-twenty hindsight and see clearly what had happened during the promotional project. The information she gathered in these exercises gave her the foundation for making changes—but before she did anything, she completed the remaining five Action Steps for Change.

12

Step #2: Map the Emotional Dynamics in Your Family

I n Step #2, you will gather the same kind of information about your family that you gathered about your office in Step #1. You'll uncover your family's secret emotional connections, roles, rules, ways of relating, stresses, strategies, and patterns of behavior—and map them in charts that mirror those you did for your office's emotional system.

Patterns that appear in both emotional systems are usually the dynamics you learned in your family and may have brought to work. These are the areas where you have power. If the family pattern is yours, then you can change that behavior to dramatically improve your relationships with people at work.

Naturally, any family's dynamics shift slightly from year to year, but in family-systems therapy we've found that general themes are consistent over time. Families that revolve around a persecuting father or a martyred mother, for instance, continue to do so decade after decade. How that dynamic affects a five-year-old is different from how it affects a twenty-year-old, but the dynamic is the same. The role of Superachiever may look different at eighteen than it does at eight, but the purpose is identical: to prove one's worth and gain attention through extraordinary accomplishment.

If you have trouble remembering how the roles, rules, ways of relating, and other emotional dynamics in your family worked, imagine a particularly stressful situation that involved the whole family: an illness, a move, financial difficulty, an unwanted marriage or pregnancy, a drug problem, a new baby, a death, etc. Think about how people acted during those times, and how they related to one another. How old were you? How did the event affect you? How did you act? In retrospect, what defenses do you believe you used?

The exercises in this chapter are designed to give you priceless information, not to provide a bludgeon with which to beat yourself up. Families are inherently stressful institutions. No one is to blame for finding tools, tactics, and defenses to counteract that stress. The point is that those tools, tactics, and defenses are rarely useful to adults in a corporate environment, and it's time to discard them. To do that, you have to identify clearly what they are. The more clearly you see them, the easier it becomes to detach from them.

We'll use my client Alice's homework to illustrate these exercises, as we did in the last chapter.

◩ ALICE'S FAMILY

The exercises in the last chapter gave Alice a good understanding of the emotional dynamics in her office. Next, she needed to find out which pieces of that office emotional baggage were hers. To discover which patterns, tactics, and dynamics she had brought to the situation, she completed the mirror exercises in this chapter. That effort pinpointed where she could make changes.

Alice's father Donald was a successful attorney who was a brilliant, aloof workaholic and almost completely absent from the family's emotional life. Alice always had the impression that he would like and approve of her if he knew her, but he was rarely home at times when she was awake. Her mother Gwen was a medical assistant who worked fairly regular hours but felt burdened by also having to run the house and manage three children. She never failed to let her children know how much she was sacrificing for them and how difficult they made her life when they didn't behave properly and do their chores on time. Even as a child, Alice realized that her mother's martyred stance was a ploy to get from them the attention and affection she lacked from her husband. Alice had contempt for this tactic and promised herself that she would never be weak or victimized. At the same time, she wanted to maintain peace in the household and win both her mother's and father's approval.

Alice's sister Nancy was two years younger than she was, and her little brother Joey was two years younger than Nancy. Nancy was the family Scapegoat, the one who was always getting into trouble. Joey was completely overpowered by his respectively supercompetent and Bad Girl older sisters. He tended to disappear and get lost in the shuffle.

Gwen had devised a system of chores for the children to ensure that the household ran according to Donald's strict, high standards even in her absence, but both Nancy and Joey resisted this system and rarely finished their many tasks on their own. Alice would have to hunt them down and bully them into getting everything done. By the time their parents walked in the door, everything was running smoothly again— but it was a struggle. Her siblings fought Alice every step of the way— Joey with tears and Nancy with screams and accusations.

Alice knew that things would fall apart quickly if she didn't take charge and steamroll her siblings into doing their work. Their mother would moan and groan and blame her for not riding herd on the kids and for getting them all in trouble with their father. Donald would be furious and leave a note revoking privileges. No one would speak for days, and all the tension would be Alice's fault. It was easier to whip Nancy and Joey into line, no matter how much they hated her. That not only prevented disaster but might actually win her some minor recognition. Her mother took most of the credit for the household running smoothly, but Alice hoped her father knew that at least some of it was her doing.

Playing the roles of Superachiever and Persecutor kept Alice from relating to her siblings with affection or respect. Joey withdrew into sullen resentment, and Nancy came to his rescue. She would often yell at Alice, "Leave the baby alone! He's done enough."

Donald's father Will lived with the family, and he also thought Alice's treatment of Nancy and Joey was criminal. They always ran to him when Alice was "mean." He would pat their heads, give them candy, and tell Alice, "Give them a break. They're only kids. You're not in charge here." Yet if anything went wrong, Alice was in charge and the blame fell squarely on her head.

▣   Uncovering this information wasn't comfortable for Alice, but it was a crucial step in making the powerful changes that she implemented later. Using her work as an example, complete the following exercises to map the emotional dynamics in your family.

▣   YOUR FAMILY GENOGRAM

A genogram is a map or diagram of the basic structure and relationships in your family. It is your family's *visible* organizational chart. Drawing this diagram may seem like a simple thing, but in family-systems therapy we find that genograms often reveal unexpected factors that influenced your development.

Instructions: Draw your family genogram, using rectangles for men and circles for women. List everyone's date of birth, death, cause of death, marriage, and divorce. Cross out the names of people who are deceased. I recommend that you go back to your grandparents, because their legacy of rules—and the roles your parents played with them—probably influenced you and the emotional patterns you learned.

This is what Alice's genogram looked like:

▣ YOUR FAMILY'S INVISIBLE WORLD

Your genogram shows relationships, but, like your company's organizational chart, it may have little connection with how people actually related to one another. The map of your family's emotional realities shows how people really related to one another and will be of greater use to you in spotting similarities between your family's dynamics and the situation at work. The more similar this map is to the Invisible Organizational Chart at work, the more likely you may be to fall into your family's old tactics and behaviors.

Instructions: Write the names of family members around the perimeter of a circle, with the women in circles and the men in rectangles, as you did in your family genogram. There may be individuals you didn't include in your genogram whom you nonetheless feel played a signifi-cant role in your family, such as a distant aunt or uncle that your parents ostracized or idolized. If you sense there is someone you need to include in this diagram who was not part of your genogram, do so.

This is Alice's map:

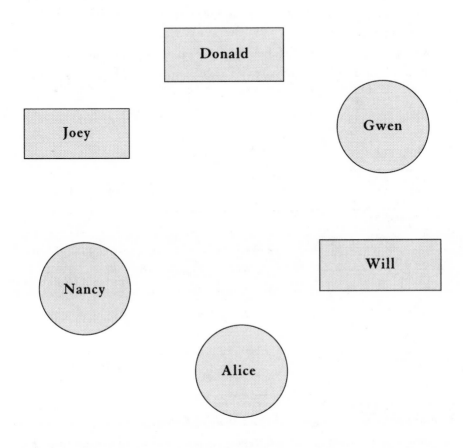

Roles in Your Family

Think about the roles that people in your family adopted, especially under stress. What role or roles did your mother play? Your father? Your brothers and sisters? What role did you play? Remember, most people play more than one role, depending on the circumstances and the people involved.

In family systems therapy, we stress that you don't have to be right about what roles your family members played. It's not uncommon for your experience of what happened to be different from your brothers' and sisters', or from your parents'. Stick to your own gut feelings and venture a guess. If you perceive your mother to have been a Persecutor and your father a Victim, you're not rendering judgment on them; you're simply identifying their behavior so that you can better understand your own.

Instructions: List the role(s) each person played, and enter them on the map of your family's invisible world. Be sure to include yourself in this list.

NAME   ROLE(S)

_____   _____

_____   _____

_____   _____

_____   _____

_____   _____

_____   _____

Here is Alice's work:

NAME	ROLE(S)
Donald	Persecutor or Tyrant
Gwen	Martyr, Victim (of Donald's intolerance)
Alice	Superachiever (to self, Donald and Gwen)
	Persecutor (to Nancy, Joey, and Will)
	Rescuer (of Gwen)
Nancy	Scapegoat, Rebel
	Rescuer (of Joey)
	Victim (of Alice)
Joey	Victim
Will	Rescuer

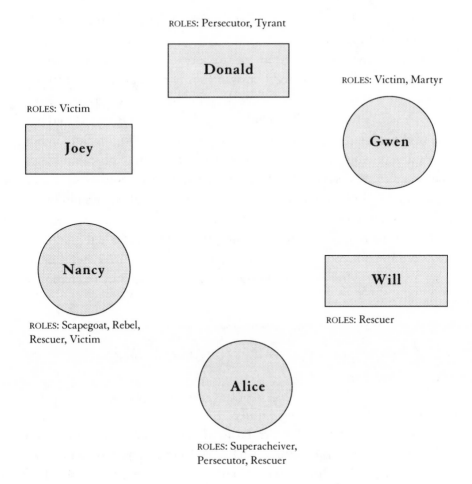

ROLES: Persecutor, Tyrant

Donald

ROLES: Victim, Martyr

ROLES: Victim

Joey

Gwen

Nancy

Will

ROLES: Scapegoat, Rebel,
Rescuer, Victim

ROLES: Rescuer

Alice

ROLES: Superacheiver,
Persecutor, Rescuer

Alice was stunned when she saw the similarities between these dynamics and what had happened at her office. Donald was the same distant Persecutor as Earl, the president of her organization. Gwen was
the same kind of ineffective intermediate authority that Rick was at
work—the one whose neck Alice had to save, but who never gave her
much credit with the higher-ups. Their styles were different—Rick
was a handwringing People Pleaser and Gwen a nastier, glummer Martyr—but their effect on Alice was similar. They were the same kind of
immediate motivator in her compulsion to make sure things got done.
Nancy and Joey were remarkably like Ed and Connie. They didn't do

things that they had agreed to do and resisted Alice when she tried to whip them into shape.

The most uncomfortable part of this exercise for Alice was seeing how closely she had recreated her own family roles at work. In stressful situations at the office—and work not getting done was one of the most stressful situations Alice could imagine—all her instincts told her to take charge and steamroll people into doing things right. Both in her family and at work, she dove into the Superachiever, Rescuer, and Persecutor roles. She saved the day, rescued the weak, and won minor recognition by bullying others, but she was not well liked and never got the kind of affection or approval she wanted.

"Is that the only way I'm ever going to be able to relate to people?" she asked me. Of course, it wasn't. She was taking positive steps to become aware of what she was doing, and that was the key to changing her behavior.

Your Family's Ways of Relating

The ways of relating you're most likely to use at work are those that were used most often in your family.

Instructions: List the ways of relating that each family member used to deal with stressful interactions such as conflict, disagreements, breaking family rules, and disobedience. Don't forget to include yourself. Enter these ways of relating on the map of your family's invisible world.

A reminder: Some of the ineffective, unhealthy ways of relating that often find their way to work are: denial, avoidance, withdrawal, attacking, manipulation, bullying, emotional bribery, placating, blaming, playing Victim, shaming, criticizing, the silent treatment, intimidation, gossiping, rescuing, domination, patronizing or condescension, threats, verbal or physical abuse.

NAME	WAYS OF RELATING
_____	_____
_____	_____
_____	_____
_____	_____
_____	_____
_____	_____

This is Alice's list:

NAME	WAYS OF RELATING
Donald	Bullying, threats, silent treatment, withdrawing
Gwen	Playing Victim, shaming, blaming
Alice	Bullying, intimidation, placating, rescuing, becoming a Superachiever
Nancy	Fighting back, verbal attacks
Joey	Silent treatment, playing Victim, holding grudges
Will	Shaming, rescuing

ROLES: Persecutor, Tyrant
WAYS OF RELATING:
Bullying, threats, silent
treatment, withdrawing

Donald

ROLES: Victim, Martyr
WAYS OF RELATING:
Playing Victim,
shaming, blaming

ROLES: Victim
WAYS OF RELATING:
Silence, playing Victim,
holding grudges

Joey

Gwen

Nancy

ROLES: Scapegoat, Rebel,
Rescuer, Victim
WAYS OF RELATING:
Fighting back, verbal
attacks

Will

ROLES: Rescuer
WAYS OF RELATING:
Shaming, rescuing

Alice

ROLES: Superacheiver,
Persecutor, Rescuer
WAYS OF RELATING:
Bullying, intimidation, pla-
cating, rescuing, super-
achieving

With each exercise, it became clearer to Alice that she was duplicat-
ing her family's tactics at work. Her automatic response to pressure
from authority to produce results was to assume that those around her
would be as incompetent and irresponsible as Nancy and Joey had
been—and to relate to them in the same ways she had related to her siblings. And it wasn't an option to do only what she was able to do—
everything had to be done perfectly.

These realizations made Alice uncomfortable, but she also saw that if it was her baggage, then she could change it. Earl would never be another Einstein, Rick was still an ineffective People Pleaser, Connie might go to her grave with a whine on her lips, and Ed with a sneer or growl on his—but there were other things in her emotional environment that Alice *could* change, and she was beginning to see what they were.

Emotional Triangles in Your Family

In family systems therapy, we believe that families are where we learn to build emotional triangles.

Instructions: List the emotional triangles in your family. Write the role each person played after his or her name, then draw these triangles on the map of emotional realities in your family.

PERSON #1 (ROLE)	PERSON #2 (ROLE)	PERSON #3 (ROLE)
_____	_____	_____
_____	_____	_____
_____	_____	_____
_____	_____	_____

Emotional triangles abounded in Alice's family:

PERSON #1 (ROLE)	PERSON #2 (ROLE)	PERSON #3 (ROLE)
Alice (Persecutor)	Joey (Victim)	Nancy (Rescuer)
Alice (Persecutor)	Nancy/Joey (Victims)	Will (Rescuer)
Donald (Persecutor)	Gwen (Victim)	Alice (Rescuer)

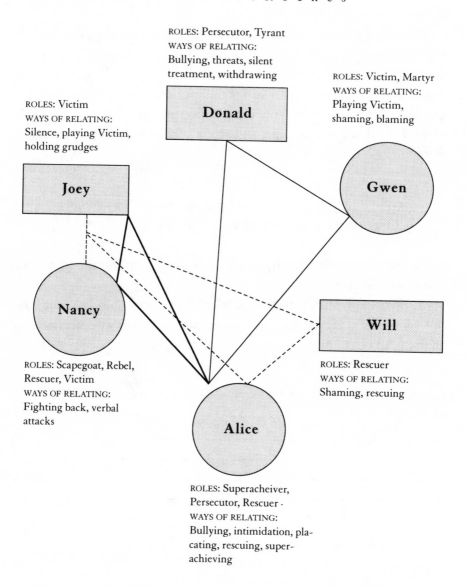

ROLES: Persecutor, Tyrant
WAYS OF RELATING:
Bullying, threats, silent
treatment, withdrawing

Donald

ROLES: Victim, Martyr
WAYS OF RELATING:
Playing Victim,
shaming, blaming

ROLES: Victim
WAYS OF RELATING:
Silence, playing Victim,
holding grudges

Joey

Gwen

Nancy

Will

ROLES: Scapegoat, Rebel,
Rescuer, Victim
WAYS OF RELATING:
Fighting back, verbal
attacks

ROLES: Rescuer
WAYS OF RELATING:
Shaming, rescuing

Alice

ROLES: Superacheiver,
Persecutor, Rescuer ·
WAYS OF RELATING:
Bullying, intimidation, pla-
cating, rescuing, super-
achieving

Alice noted in this exercise that she was never the Victim, even though she often felt victimized by her situation at work. Victim was the role her mother had played, and Alice had vowed never to be like that. She couldn't permit herself the weakness she perceived in Victims; she had to keep running, keep producing, always one step ahead of trouble. (Nevertheless, I contend she was a covert Victim with the situation itself as Persecutor and no Rescuer in sight.)

Now set your diagram aside and use a separate sheet of paper to complete your assessment of rules and mixed messages in your family.

◘ YOUR FAMILY'S RULES

This exercise will help you determine which of the rules at work are your company's, and which you may have thought were your company's but actually originated in your family.

To help you start thinking about your family's invisible rules, here are some common unstated rules in families:

- It's not okay to disagree; just be nice. You'll be safe as long as you're good.

- Only parents can be angry.

- You have to look good; you can be yourself as long as you keep up appearances.

- Keep your feelings to yourself. Don't ask questions or upset people.

- Don't talk about yourself or feel good about yourself; it's selfish.

Use these questions to start thinking about your family's unwritten rules:

- *What topics couldn't you bring up?* Money? Sex? Authority? A family member or relative's drinking or drug use? Other family problems?

- *Did you have to hide any of your activities or beliefs?* This applies not only to religious, sociological, and political views and activities but also to preferences and personal taste.

- *How did your family deal with unpleasant feelings such as anger, sadness, hurt, shame, confusion, and fear?* Were you encouraged to tell your parents that you were upset or angry? Were you allowed to cry openly?

* *Was there a need to avoid upsetting or angering one of your parents?* Would you tiptoe around your father at night while he was reading the paper or having a drink? If something happened to you, could you tell your parents?

Instructions: List your family's invisible rules. Watch for ways these rules are duplicated in your workplace today—or for ways in which you unconsciously follow them even though they are not in place at your job.

Don't be surprised if you find only a few rules at first. Most of us got so used to operating by our families' unspoken, invisible rules that it's hard to verbalize exactly what they were. On the other hand, you may be shocked at how rigid some of your family's rules were, and at the degree to which following them was more important than being happy or solving the family's problems.

Invisible Rules in My Family:

* _____

* _____

* _____

* _____

* _____

* _____

These were some of Alice's family's rules:

Invisible Rules in My Family:
* Everyone and everything must be perfect at all times.

* Dad is the boss; we all do what he wants.

* If you don't obey the rules, you won't get affection or approval. You have to earn your place in the family.

Alice was amazed how similar these rules were to the rules by which she lived at the office and had to reconsider whether anyone at work had actually imposed them on her.

◘ MIXED MESSAGES IN YOUR FAMILY

The party line rarely reflects reality in families. Some common mixed messages (with the reality stated in parentheses) are:

* We're one big happy family, and we all love one another (*except for that stony silence between Mom and Dad, the black eye that Ray gave Timmy, and Debbie running away because she was convinced nobody cared about her*).

* We can tell each other anything (*except if it's unpleasant or threatening*).

* Tell your parents when you're in trouble (*if you want to get into more trouble*).

* No one here has any problems (*unless you count Mom's pills, Dad's workaholism, Terri's failing grades, or Alex's fistfights on the playground*).

Instructions: Make a list of the mixed messages that dominated your family.

Mixed Messages in My Family:
* _____

* _____

* _____

* _____

* _____

* _____

* _____

Here is Alice's list:

Mixed Messages in My Family:
* We all work together supportively to make the household run smoothly (*except Alice is to blame when things aren't done*).

- Mom and Dad care about and treat all the children equally (*except Mom prefers Joey*).

- It's who you are that matters, not what you do (*except you'd better be successful*).

In fact, nobody in Alice's family had worked together; almost everyone was at cross-purposes. Gwen cared much more about Joey than she did about the girls. What you did was much more important than who you were, and Alice was treated very differently from the other children.

When Alice came across mixed messages at the safety council, she capitulated without batting an eye. They were old hat, simply the way life was; it never occurred to her to clarify them. She expected mixed messages and took them in her stride. She wasn't even aware of the stress they caused, or how they prevented her from dealing directly with problems.

▣ COMPARING THE INVISIBLE WORLDS AT HOME AND WORK

You now have clear pictures of the invisible worlds at work and in your family. Take a moment to compare the diagrams and lists, as Alice did. Where are they similar? These are your areas of power, the situations you are best able to change because they probably involve your own family patterns.

Based on the work you've done on Step #1 and Step #2, in which you mapped the emotional dynamics in your office and family, answer these questions:

- What family patterns have you brought to work?

- Which are the strongest patterns you have identified?

- Have you seen anything you'd like to change about yourself as a result of these exercises?

Alice saw that she was playing the same oppressive Persecutor role with colleagues Ed and Connie that she had with Nancy and Joey. Her relationship with the president of the company, Earl, was similar to her relationship with her distant, demanding father. She related to her boss, Rick, as she had to her mother. Rick and her mother were trying to placate someone higher up (Earl and Alice's father) who insisted on perfection and control and put her unofficially in charge of others for whom they were actually responsible.

Alice allowed this to happen because the role of Superachiever helped her manage stress by feeling more in control. She did it well, it kept her and everybody else out of trouble, she got attention for saving the day, and she had built her identity on being "the best one" who never got properly acknowledged. That role was comfortable for her because she'd been playing it all her life, even though it had become counterproductive at work. Bullying people also was a lifelong habit, since others who didn't do their work properly represented a threat that she would fail.

Alice could look back and see that these same dynamics had come into play on previous jobs, but she had never been consciously aware of them or examined their origin. She had just assumed that she was always surrounded by wimpy bosses and mean-spirited or incompetent coworkers. Recognizing that she played an active part in what was going on gave her the power to change the situation.

In the next chapter, you will assess the risks, consider various changes to improve relationships at work, and examine the consequences of each one.

13

Step #3: Assess the Risks

N ow that you know which of your family patterns most strongly affect your relationships at work, you can start exploring what changes you want to make. Before you do anything, however, it's important to assess the risks involved.

▣ WHAT YOU CAN CHANGE, WHAT YOU CAN'T

Some of my clients want to plunge headlong into change. An important part of assessing risk is understanding these three Truths About Change:

• *You can't change another person's thoughts or feelings, no matter how much power or influence you have over that person.* People who need others to change in order for problems to get solved give away all their power and usually wind up feeling angry and frustrated. If you start with the premise that you can only change your own thoughts, feelings, and behavior, you are far ahead of the game.

- *You may influence another's behavior but only temporarily.* If your colleague is chronically late with information you need to do your work and that person likes and respects you, then you may get temporary results by saying, "Sharon, I'd really appreciate your getting me that material by Tuesday. It would be a big help to me. Thanks." Don't expect permanent changes, however, unless Sharon is actively committed to changing her pattern of being late.

- *You can change your experience of a work relationship by changing the way you function in it.* If you stop playing the Victim with Suzie, or stop letting Alan hook you into his power games, your experience of those relationships will change. You probably won't feel as anxious, limited, or frustrated as you did. It's something you can do unilaterally, without Suzie or Alan's cooperation, to regain your self-respect and a certain level of control.

It boils down to this: You can always make internal changes, and those changes will affect how you feel in a relationship or situation. Sometimes, but not always, they will affect how other people behave or the situation itself.

When you move one piece of a mobile, all the other pieces move along with it to find a new balance. The whole arrangement of the mobile changes. When you make internal changes, you move around at least one piece in the mobile of your office's emotional environment. The rest have to shift to find their positions in the new balance. You can't control where those other pieces land, but you can put the mobile in motion.

At the very least, moving your piece removes you from the entanglement of unhealthy dynamics and gives you peace of mind. It may or may not result in other people acting differently.

◼ RISK VS. URGENCY

Deciding what you want to change in your work relationships is a serious, strategic process. You need to know exactly why you want the change, how much you want it, and how risky it will be.

169

The next three exercises will give you that information. The first exercise pinpoints which of your work relationships are most stressful and why. It will suggest the kinds of changes you may want to make. The second exercise charts how much influence each person has over you and how much room there is for change in that relationship. It will tell you exactly how risky change will be with each person. The third deals with the general levels of stress and flexibility in your workplace and tells you how risky it will be to make any change in your office.

We will use my client Alice's exercises as examples, as we did in Chapters 11 and 12. You may want to get out the Invisible Organizational Chart of your workplace that you created in Chapter 11 and use it as a reference.

◙ EXERCISE #1: THE URGENCY FACTOR: WHO IS MOST STRESSFUL?

If the basic desires to feel included, competent, and liked, which we discussed in Chapter 2, are being met in your interaction with someone, then that relationship probably feels pleasant, easy, healthy, and productive. If they are not being met, then you're likely to experience some degree of stress, difficulty, and discomfort.

In this exercise, you'll look at what your expectations are of various people at work in terms of feeling included, competent, and liked; at what you are actually getting from them in these areas; and at what you would honestly like from them.

The level of stress in each relationship depends on how much difference there is between what you're getting and what you want, and also on how important that person is to you. The more important he or she is, the greater your desires to feel included, competent, and liked—and the greater your frustration if those desires are not met. Whenever you feel dissatisfied with a work relationship, there is probably some discrepancy between how you want to feel around that person, and how you actually do feel.

When you know why you feel frustrated and let down around certain individuals, you can do something about it—either by talking with them or by changing your own attitudes and expectations. You may find, for instance, that you've been trying to get emotional desires met in relationships in which it's not really possible to do so, no matter how hard you try and no matter what you do.

These exercises are modified from Will Schutz's surveys for inclusion, control and openness. Use the following scale to determine the degree to which you agree or disagree with the statements in the exercises:

DEGREE OF AGREEMENT

Disagree   Agree
0   1   2   3   4   5   6   7   8   9

You'll make three separate charts to indicate how your relationships with each individual on your Invisible Organizational Chart fulfills your three basic desires to be included, competent, and liked.

Feeling Included

Feeling included suggests belonging, associating with others, sharing information, joining in, being involved, having contact, participating, and experiencing status. The feelings associated with it are respect, recognition, significance, and being "in" rather than "out." When your need to feel included is not met, you may feel ignored, left out, forgotten, or neglected.

Instructions: Fill out the following chart, with the names of people at work across the top. Assign a number to Statements A and B, depending on how strongly you agree or disagree with the statements. Then subtract the Statement B number from the Statement A number. This gives you the degree to which your desire to feel included is, or is not, being met with that particular individual.

	IN MY RELATIONSHIP WITH:						
A	I am included and feel significant						
B	I want to be included and feel significant						
	A-B=Satisfaction						

Here is what Alice's chart looked like:

		IN MY RELATIONSHIP WITH:						
		EARL	RICK	CONNIE	ED	MARCIA	SARAH	YVONNE
A	I am included and feel significant	3	7	5	3	9	6	3
B	I want to be included and feel significant	9	9	5	5	7	3	3
	A-B=Satisfaction	-6	-2	0	-2	2	3	0

This chart revealed to Alice that she wanted a great deal of inclusion from Earl but was not getting it. She also wanted a high level from Rick but was getting more from him than she was from Earl. From Connie, Marcia, and Yvonne, she was getting just as much inclusion as she wanted. She wanted slightly more from Ed, but her desired level of inclusion from him was only 5, not particularly high, and so that lack didn't have much impact on her.

Feeling Competent

Feeling competent means having control over your work and influence over the people and issues that affect you. It suggests confidence and power. When your desire to feel competent isn't being met, you may feel humiliated, powerless, inadequate, or out of control.

Instructions: Fill out the following chart, as you did above.

		IN MY RELATIONSHIP WITH:						
A	I am in control and feel competent							
B	I want to be in control and feel competent							
	A-B=Satisfaction							

Here is Alice's chart:

		IN MY RELATIONSHIP WITH:						
		EARL	RICK	CONNIE	ED	MARCIA	SARAH	YVONNE
A	I am in control and feel competent	5	8	6	4	9	5	5
B	I want to be in control and feel competent	9	9	9	9	9	6	5
	A-B=Satisfaction	-4	-1	-3	-5	0	-1	0

It was no surprise to Alice that she had a high need to feel competent and in control or that her relationships with Earl, Ed, and Connie—with whom she experienced the greatest difference between the control she was getting and what she wanted—were the most stressful. Again, she felt frustrated because she didn't think Earl understood how competent she was. She had a high desire for control over Marcia, which was being met, and a relatively low need for control over Yvonne, which was also being met. No one had much control over Sarah, but her impact on Alice was minimal. Her high level of control over Rick grew out of his dependence on her to produce results that kept Earl off his back.

Feeling Liked

Feeling liked means being able to disclose your true thoughts and feelings to others without punishment. It means feeling openhearted, accepted, accepting, honest, and appreciated. When the desire to be liked is not met, you may feel rejected, unlikable, put off, distant, judged, or disliked.

Instructions: Fill out the following chart.

IN MY RELATIONSHIP WITH:						
A I am open and feel liked						
B I want to be open and feel liked						
A-B=Satisfaction						

This is Alice's chart:

IN MY RELATIONSHIP WITH:						
A I am open and feel liked						
B I want to be open and feel liked						
A-B=Satisfaction						

Again, the problems were Earl, Connie, and Ed. She thought Earl liked her well enough, but her need to feel liked by him was high. Her desire to be liked by Ed and Connie was based primarily on her need to get results from them, so their influence over her wasn't as great as it would have been if she honestly wanted to be liked and respected by them. What she was getting from Rick nearly matched her desire. Marcia, as always, was a loyal supporter. Alice's desire to be liked by Sarah and Yvonne was minimal and was closely matched by the reality.

These exercises helped Alice pinpoint exactly where she wanted to make changes: Earl, Ed, Connie, and Rick. Review your own charts to determine which relationships are most stressful for you and where you want to start making changes. In the next exercises, you'll see if those particular changes are prudent—or if they may be too risky. It's always best to start with easy, safer changes and work your way up to more difficult or risky ones.

◙ EXERCISE #2: THE RISK FACTOR: WHO IS MOST DIFFICULT?

This exercise tells you how risky it will be to make changes in each of your relationships at work. It charts how much influence people have over you (either because they have power in the organization or because you care what they think of you) against how much room for change and growth there is in that particular relationship.

Emotional Influence

As you read the following questions, think about the people in your office. Notice who comes to mind most often and who has the most influence over your thoughts, feelings, and behavior.

Who are the most important people to you at work? Why are they important? Do they hold purse strings? Do you admire them and want them to like you? Who do you most want to support you and acknowledge your work efforts?

Who makes you most anxious? Upset? Frustrated? Whom do you intentionally avoid? Whom do you trust? People who provide a safe place to share your thoughts and feelings can become extremely important to you. Whose feelings are you most afraid of hurting? The more concerned you are about someone's reactions, the more your be-havior is influenced by what that person's reactions may be.

The people whose names came up in response to these questions are the ones who have emotional influence over you. Write down the names of each person on your Invisible Organizational Chart and indicate the degree of influence each has over your thoughts, feelings, and behav-ior: high, moderate, or low.

NAME   EMOTIONAL INFLUENCE

_____   _____
_____   _____
_____   _____
_____   _____
_____   _____

Alice came up with this list:

NAME	EMOTIONAL INFLUENCE
Earl	High
Rick	Moderate
Ed	High
Connie	Moderate
Marcia	Moderate
Sarah	Low
Yvonne	Low

Flexibility

Flexibility in a relationship means that both of you can change and grow without jeopardizing the connection, that you can talk about your relationship, and that you can make adjustments in it when needed. Think about the people at work as you ask yourself: Who is most de-fensive when you talk with them openly about problems in your rela-tionship with them? Whom do you experience as demanding and controlling when confronted with uncomfortable issues? These people have a low level of flexibility.

Who listens to your concerns and responds respectfully? To whom can you bring work problems without fear of being ignored, blamed, resented, or criticized? Who do you feel is most open to acknowledging their own feelings and thoughts in a conflict—without blaming you or others? These people usually have a moderate to high degree of flexibility.

Instructions: List the people at work and write down their level of flexibility: high, moderate, or low.

NAME   FLEXIBILITY

_____   _____

_____   _____

_____   _____

_____   _____

_____   _____

This is Alice's list:

NAME	FLEXIBILITY
Earl	Low
Rick	High
Ed	Moderate
Connie	High
Marcia	High
Sarah	Moderate
Yvonne	Low

Your Most Difficult Relationships

Now that you've assessed the levels of emotional influence and flexibility in each of your work relationships, you can put these two sets of information together to determine how difficult it will be to change how you behave with each person.

Instructions: Fill in the following chart, plotting each person's influence over you against his or her flexibility. List your coworkers along the side of the graph in order of flexibility and along the top of the graph in order of influence. Make a point on the graph where each person's level of influence and flexibility intersect, and notice the quadrant in which it appears.

FLEXIBILITY	INFLUENCE		
	Low	Mod	High
High	Quadrant #2		Quadrant #3
Mod	Quadrant #1		Quadrant #4
Low			

This is Alice's graph:

FLEXIBILITY		INFLUENCE		
		Low	Mod	High
		Yvonne Sarah Marcia Connie Rick Ed Earl		
High	Marcia	Quadrant #2 M.		Quadrant #3
	Connie	C.		
	Rick		R.	
	Ed		Ed.	
Mod	Sarah	Quadrant #1		Quadrant #4
	Yvonne	S.		
	Earl	Y.		Earl
Low				

Here's how to use the graph to assess how challenging it will be to make changes in each of these relationships:

Quadrant #1 (low to moderate flexibility; low to moderate emotional influence): People in this quadrant are fairly rigid, so they may trigger your family patterns and be unwilling to resolve differences or accommodate change. On the other hand, their influence over you is low, so these may not be your most stressful relationships. Minor changes are possible here, but proceed with caution and remember that they may not be worth the risk. The best strategy is often to spend less time and energy worrying about these people's opinion of you.

Quadrant #2 (moderate to high flexibility; low to moderate emotional influence): These people are not likely to trigger defensive family patterns, and their flexibility makes changes relatively safe and easy. These are often casual relationships with little interaction beyond completing tasks.

If you are a supervisor, some of the people you manage may fall into this category. You may need them to do their work, but you are only minimally concerned about what they think of you. If you treat these people with the same respect that you expect from them, you'll create an open and productive emotional environment.

Relationships with coworkers that fall into this category are often relatively pleasant and safe. You probably enjoy a good rapport and working friendship. They represent a good opportunity to make changes without seriously jeopardizing your job or causing too much stress for yourself.

Quadrant #3 (moderate to high flexibility; moderate to high emotional influence): Although the emotional influence in these relationships is fairly high, they are resilient and flexible. Changes are possible if you are careful. Family patterns may be triggered but can be worked through if you are prepared. These are often connections with coworkers or supervisors with whom you share a pleasant, open connection. They are similar to the relationships in Quadrant 2, except that you care more what these people think and feel about you.

Quadrant #4 (low to moderate flexibility; moderate to high emotional influence): These are high-risk relationships that carry the greatest potential for triggering defensive family dynamics—and the lowest potential for working through them. You experience the people who fall into this quadrant as rigid, with only a minimal ability to tolerate the kinds of changes you may want to make. These relationships are often with supervisors or coworkers who can have a direct impact on your career, job satisfaction, or self-esteem. *Proceed very cautiously if you make any changes with people in this quadrant, and don't start here.*

Where to Start

The most difficult relationships are those that fall in Quadrants #1 and 4. The least difficult are those in Quadrants #2 and #3. You'll be tempted to start with the relationships in Quadrant #4, because those people have the most influence over you and represent the greatest source of stress—but expect considerable stress if you change your behavior in Quadrant #4 relationships.

I recommend that you begin with Quadrant #2, where you are least likely to encounter defensive reactions, and work your way slowly through Quadrant #3, then Quadrant #1, to the most difficult people in Quadrant #4. This sequence lets you begin with the easiest, least stressful changes and practice with increasingly difficult relationships so that you get some experience before taking on the most challenging connections.

▣ EXERCISE #3: HOW RISKY IS *ANY* CHANGE IN YOUR COMPANY?

By now, you probably have a general understanding of how stressful, and how rigid, the emotional environment is in your company. This exercise will give you some idea of how risky it will be to make changes of any kind.

How Stressful Is Your Company?

We've seen that high, chronic stress keeps people from doing their jobs well, solving problems, and relating to one another in productive ways. The conditions listed below are present in all workplaces from time to time, but when they persist they are symptoms of chronic stress. Take this quiz to determine the level of stress in your company. Score one point for each yes answer.

YES	NO	
____	____	Sick days and sick leave are abused.
____	____	People deny problems, even though avoiding them affects their work and creates more problems.
____	____	Communication between supervisors and employees is confusing and riddled with mixed messages.
____	____	High turnover is denied or rationalized.
____	____	Rules and policies are inconsistent.
____	____	Conflicts are not worked through and reconciled.
____	____	Management mistakes are denied.
____	____	People are scapegoated.
____	____	Management is more interested in short-term relief than in long-term solutions to problems.
____	____	Mistrust pervades the workplace.
____	____	Everyone knows that everyone is pretending there are no problems.
____	____	The same kinds of problems keep cropping up.

NUMBER OF YES ANSWERS: ____

Circle the number of yes answers to determine the level of stress in your workplace:

LOW			MODERATE			HIGH			CHRONIC		
1	2	3	4	5	6	7	8	9	10	11	12

How Rigid Is Your Company?

As the rigidity of the emotional environment in your workplace increases, you will observe more of the following characteristics. Score one point for each yes answer.

YES   NO

YES	NO	
____	____	Differences of opinion mean lack of loyalty, not opportunities for creativity and improvement.
____	____	Secrets and emotional triangles abound.
____	____	Nonessential paperwork increases as people try to protect themselves from being scapegoated.
____	____	Conflicts and tension are denied and avoided.
____	____	Management shares little information with employees until a crisis occurs.
____	____	People feel that they have little control over their jobs.
____	____	Management's primary focus is maintaining the status quo. It must control everything and cannot delegate responsibility or authority.
____	____	Getting the job done is more important than people's mental or physical well-being.
____	____	Talking about problems is considered troublemaking.
____	____	New ways of doing things are suspect.
____	____	People feel like cogs in the wheels of machinery.

NUMBER OF YES ANSWERS:____

Circle the number of yes answers to determine the level of rigidity in your workplace:

LOW			MODERATE				HIGH			CHRONIC	
1	2	3	4	5	6	7	8	9	10	11	12

Instructions: Add the numbers you circled to reflect the stress and rigidity in your workplace. The total of these two numbers is____. *The higher your total score,* the less effective your organization or workplace is in dealing with external and internal problems and the stress of change. If you sense that your organization is even less able to deal with stress than the actual score reflects, go with your intuition and circle a higher number.

ORGANIZATIONAL EFFECTIVENESS IN DEALING
WITH CHANGE

HIGH					MODERATE						LOW
2	4	6	8	10	12	14	16	18	20	22	24

Alice scored the level of stress in her workplace at 8 and the level of rigidity at 10. Her total was 18, so her organization's effectiveness in dealing with change was moderate to low. That meant that change would be possible in the organization but that she would have to be cautious.

The more ineffective the emotional system at your workplace, the more difficult or risky it will be to introduce changes. If your workplace has high or chronic stress and high rigidity, then move slowly in following the Six Action Steps for Change—and expect some discomfort.

I know of two people who ignored this advice. They were frustrated with their work situations and made quick changes in how they related to people in Quadrants 1 and 4. One, a commercial artist, got fired shortly after accusing his supervisor of taking the credit for a new design. The other, an executive secretary, was told to back off or she would lose her job. They were both working in highly stressful, inflexible systems. Any changes threatened both their supervisors and the system itself.

It's important to be enthusiastic about the changes you want to make, but it's equally important to go about those changes in an intelligent, reasonable, well-planned way that has the best chance of succeeding. In the next chapter, you'll target the specific family patterns you want to change.

14

Step #4: Choose Your Changes

In Action Steps #1 and #2, you pinpointed the specific family patterns that you bring to the office. In Step #3, you looked more closely at the risks involved in making changes. In Step #4, you will use all this information to decide what specific patterns you want to change and what you want to do differently.

◨ WHAT ARE YOUR OPTIONS?

Before you choose your changes, lay out all your options. First, review your answers to the exercises in Steps #1–3. Then write the names of three or four people with whom changes seem both important and possible at the top of separate sheets of paper. Next, write under each person's name:

• *My Pattern:* What roles, rules, ways of relating, and other family patterns do I slip into with this person?

* *What I Could Change:* What could I change within myself to improve the situation?

* *The Urgency Factor:* How effectively are my emotional desires to feel included, competent, and liked being met with this person?

* *The Risk Factor:* How stressful and risky are changes with this person? There is a risk factor in any change you make within an organizational system. A key objective of the change process outlined here is to help you minimize this risk factor, by identifying and better understanding the degree of those risks.

My client Alice's candidates were, of course, Rick, Earl, Ed, and Connie. This is her work:

Earl

My Pattern: I relate to Earl as I did to my father. I'm a Secret Superachiever who makes sure that everything happens his way but who never gets credit for it. Then I feel frustrated, unappreciated, resentful, and somewhat victimized because I want his approval but have no direct access to him and let Rick take all the credit.

What I Could Change: The Superachiever role is causing me more trouble than it's worth, and I have to let it go. The Secret Superachiever role is even worse, because I don't get credit for what I do. If Earl is the one dictating what I have to do, I want a direct relationship with him.

Urgency Factor: My desires to be included, competent, and liked got satisfaction levels of −6, −4, and −3, respectively. I'm getting very little of what I want from Earl, so the Urgency Factor is high.

Risk Factor: Earl is in Quadrant #4, extremely difficult and risky for me. It wouldn't be a good idea to start with him.

Rick

My Pattern: I play the role of Superachiever and Rescuer with Rick, just as I did with Mom. I let him coerce me into managing people for whom he is actually responsible, save him from Earl's potential disapproval, then feel martyred because he steals all the credit.

What I Could Change: I want to give up the Superachiever role and stop rescuing Rick. I want to tell him that: (1) I will no longer manage people for whom he is responsible; (2) I want him to let Earl know about the good work I do; and (3) I will no longer charge in on a white horse at the last minute and get everything done.

Urgency Factor: My desires to be included, competent, and liked got satisfaction levels of −2, −1, and −1, respectively. I'm getting only slightly less than I want from him, so the Urgency Factor is fairly low—but he is my direct superior and plays a pivotal position in the office drama.

Risk Factor: Rick is in the Quadrant #3, moderate to high flexibility, moderate to high influence. Changes are possible if I proceed carefully. Rick is important to me because he's my boss, but I don't have an enormous investment in what he thinks of me and am not afraid of him. His flexibility is particularly high with me, so he may accept changes rather than be in conflict with me.

Ed

My Pattern: My pattern with Ed is the same as with my sister Nancy. I bully and intimidate him even more than I do Connie because I perceive him as stronger and better able to withstand it, and also because he fights back and I have to come down even harder.

What I Could Change: I can make a conscious effort to treat both Ed and Connie with respect, which will be much easier when I'm no longer responsible for their results. Being a Tyrant with Ed is just a habitual reaction to having my competence threatened.

Urgency Factor: My desires to be included, competent, and liked got satisfaction levels of −2, −5, and −5, respectively. Again, I'm not getting much of what I want from Ed, but his influence over me is low and will get even lower when I'm not "managing" him.

Risk Factor: Ed is in Quadrant #3, moderate to low risk.

Connie

My Pattern: Connie is my Joey. What I perceive as her sniveling, victimized incompetence threatens my ability to produce miracles. I react as a Tyrant and feel immediate pressure to whip her into shape. I don't like myself for doing that, and I blame her.

What I Could Change: I have to let go of that Tyrant role for my own sake; it's making me lose self-respect. I don't like seeing myself bully and intimidate people. It invites animosity and isn't consistent with the person I want to be.

Urgency Factor: My desires to be included, competent, and liked got satisfaction levels of 0, −3, and −5, respectively. I don't feel well liked by Connie, but her level of influence over me is low. If I let go of being responsible for her getting her work done, it will be almost none.

Risk Factor: Connie is also in Quadrant #3, a fairly low risk.

◘ MAKING THE CHOICE

Remember, you don't have to make all these changes right away. It's important to start slowly, beginning with the easiest, most flexible relationships and working toward the harder ones as you gain experience.

To choose what change to make first, consider the positive impact that the change will have on your situation at work, how risky that change is, and whether or not you feel you're ready to make the appropriate adjustments in your own attitudes and behaviors.

Alice saw that it was important for her to improve her relationship with Earl, but that his high level of influence and his low level of flexibility made changes with him extremely dangerous. She decided not to risk that right away, and to put those changes on hold for the moment.

Alice chose to start with Rick. She wanted to establish a strong new relationship with her immediate boss before she shifted any of the other pieces in the mobile. It was insurance for her job, and she also realized that much of what she wanted from Rick would affect her relationships with Ed and Connie as well. Getting her new relationship with him in place first would put her on firmer ground with them.

Changes in her relationship with Rick were only moderately risky. He was more flexible than Connie or Ed, there wasn't as great a difference between what she wanted from him and what she was getting, and she knew she had a high level of influence over him. She was more than ready to make the internal changes she had considered with Rick. She was tired of doing his work for him and willing to give up the Rescuer and Superachiever roles in order to step out of that debilitating downward cycle.

�« MAKING A PLAN

To make changes effectively, you need a specific plan of action. Your plan may include shifts in both attitudes and behaviors, and it helps to be explicit about both. Write down the exact Changes in Attitude you want to make in your attitude, any To Do's you listed in your What I Could Change sections, and a general description of the Changes for Later that may not be practical now but that you want to keep in mind.

Alice wrote of the changes she wanted to make with Rick:

Changes in Attitude: I want to do my own work well and let Rick worry about Connie and Ed's work. I don't want to resort to the Superachiever or Rescuer roles for self-esteem or approval.

To Do's: I want a meeting with Rick to sort out the lines of communication, responsibility, and authority, and to make it clear that he manages Ed and Connie and that I'm no longer willing to jump in during emergencies and save the day. I'll set that up on Monday. Then I want Rick to sit down with Connie, Ed, and me to make sure we all understand the new regime.

Changes for Later: I want him to tell Earl about my good work, but that's a separate issue and may be too much to handle right away. I'll see how these first changes go and bring it up later.

�« MAKING THE CHOICE *NOT* TO CHANGE

Give yourself permission not to change the patterns in your work relationships immediately. Many of your initial changes may be strictly internal. You don't have to discuss your plans with your boss in front of the whole company in order to make progress.

Rod, a textile designer supervised by a workaholic boss, decided it was too risky to set limits with his boss on working overtime. Instead, he worked internally on his Victim role. He wrote in his notebook each day after work about specific times during the day when he might have fallen into it but didn't, and also about those times when he got stuck in the old pattern. Simply by becoming more aware of his tendency to play that role and by taking stock each evening, he was able to let it go gradually.

Rod also took practical steps to make work more pleasant and to plan his free time better. He scheduled lunches with friends, looked for ways to become more creative in his designs, and focused on all the extra money he was making. Even though he continued to work more than he wanted, Rod felt relieved to have made the decision not to challenge his boss directly. He had eliminated the anxiety of stewing about whether or not to do so and could relax. He knew exactly what the situation was going to be and could take other steps to improve it.

Sometimes the best choice is not to challenge the patterns in stressful relationships if the negative consequences may outweigh the positive potential. The key word is *choice*.

Now that you've decided what changes you want to make, *stop!* Don't lift a finger until you've done Step #5 and planned for the resistance you will inevitably encounter.

15

Step #5: Plan for Resistance

When you start making changes, you may think you're doing something constructive and healthy—changing old habits and discarding ineffective family patterns—but other people may interpret your behavior quite differently.

When you break the invisible rules that govern relationships in your workplace, your behavior may upset people. If you stop tearing down your boss during coffee breaks with coworkers instead of engaging your family pattern of criticizing people behind their backs, you may be branded a teacher's pet. If you report a supervisor's intimidating and disrespectful behavior instead of knuckling under as you were taught to do in your family, you may lose your chance for a promotion.

You'll know how to respond appropriately to this resistance and still make your changes if you prepare by doing Action Step #5: Anticipate others' resistance and plan for it.

▣ EXPECT RESISTANCE

I can tell you, based on years of experience, that resistance isn't a matter of *if*—it's a matter of *when* and *what kind*. You will encounter resistance; count on it and plan for it.

Terry was the production manager at a small publishing company and decided that his work relationships would improve if he stopped creating emotional triangles, which had been a primary dynamic in his family. The first change he made was to stop getting involved in lunchtime conversations about the editorial director, Kendall—but he didn't anticipate others' reactions and he had no plan for handling them. He simply said he wouldn't talk about Kendall unless he was present, and walked away.

Several of Terry's coworkers ignored him for days. The publicity director actually created some triangles directed against Terry. The marketing director asked if he thought he was better than the rest of them. The teasing and backbiting lasted for several weeks, until Terry realized his mistake and corrected it. He told people he had taken my seminar and seen that talking about Kendall behind his back was making him less effective, and so he was trying to stop—but that he'd neglected to let them in on his plan, that he was sorry for that omission, and that he hoped they would support him in his resolve.

The results surprised Terry. When he took the time to deal with people's resistance, they had far fewer problems with his changes. He could have saved himself weeks of discomfort by taking that step before, rather than after, he made his changes. Anticipating other people's resistance is more than a respectful, cooperative thing to do; it can save you trouble and misunderstandings, and perhaps even your job.

▣ HOW WILL YOU REACT TO CHANGE?

Changing old family patterns can make you happier, healthier, more productive, and more successful at work—but it can also be uncomfortable. Expect resistance from yourself, as well as from others. It's our nature to resist upsetting the equilibrium, and change is an unbalancing process—internally as well as externally.

People have a wide range of responses to the prospect of changing habits that no longer work for them. Some are elated that they're finally going to do something. Others are terrified. Many people are both. Often, these feelings don't surface until it's actually time to take action.

You probably have a sense of how open you are, or are not, to change. Do you have trouble with new people at work, or with new responsibilities? (Ask yourself, If your company moved to new offices, would it be a disaster or just a new route to work?) Do you like to maintain the status quo, or do you find new challenges exciting?

There are no right answers to these questions, but it's important to anticipate how you yourself will react when you start making changes and to make contingency plans.

▣ HOW TO ANTICIPATE RESISTANCE

If you anticipate and plan for the resistance, it won't defeat you. Here's how to proceed: Write the names of all the people with whom you plan to make changes—now or later— at the tops of separate pieces of paper. Next, write what you think their reactions will be to your changes and your plan to smooth the way and make their reactions easier for you to deal with. Don't forget to include yourself among the resisters.

My client Alice realized that her tendency to adopt the role of Superachiever and Rescuer and then slide into the Tyrant stance with underlings in order to produce those miracles was at the core of many of her difficulties. It was the fundamental dynamic in all her work relationships, and letting go of it would represent a major shift—for herself and everyone around her.

These are the reactions that Alice thought Rick, Ed, Connie, and she herself might have to the changes she wanted to make—and her plans to minimize that resistance. (Although Alice decided to concentrate her efforts on her relationship with Rick initially, her plans for Ed, Connie, and herself are also laid out here to illustrate what she did.)

Rick

His Reaction: Rick's reaction will depend on how I present these proposals. If he thinks I'm trying to steamroll him, dump the problems with Ed and Connie in his lap, steal his thunder with Earl, or suggest that he doesn't manage the department well, he will get defensive and turn on me. He might explode, or he could quietly undermine me so seriously that I wouldn't have a job in six months.

My Plan: The key is to be nonthreatening, using "I" words as much as I can. I'll start by telling him about my tendency to rush to the rescue, whether or not it's my job to do so, and say I think that behavior is causing a lot of stress for all of us and would like his support in letting go of it. I'll say I think Ed and Connie will do a better job if he manages them, because I have no real authority over them and they rightly resent my bossing them around, and that I think we need a meeting with Ed and Connie to clarify the lines of communication and authority.

Ed

His Reaction: Ed is still very angry about the promotional project. He looks at me and sees red. I want to approach him in a nonthreatening way so that I don't trigger his anger and get into one of our screaming fights.

My Plan: I'll tell him that I'm no happier than he is about what's going on between us, say I'm sorry for my part in it, and tell him I want us to be equal colleagues. I'll make it clear that I don't want to manage him anymore and am willing to stick to my own business. My strongest selling point with him is that he doesn't like the situation either—and by then we will have had the four-way meeting with Rick to clarify the lines of authority.

Connie

Her Reaction: Connie may get sullen and withdrawn. In the worst case, she will refuse to believe me when I say I want a more supportive, respectful relationship and don't want to manage her anymore.

My Plan: I will be nonthreatening and quiet, try to establish a connection with her, apologize for my behavior, and tell her I want us all just to concentrate on our own work from now on.

Myself

My Reaction: If Ed and Connie aren't getting their work done, I'll be tempted to jump in and fix it. When I get stressed, my tendency will be to revert to that old pattern, to rush in and shape them up.

My Plan: I'll keep a notebook where I write every morning before work about my determination to stay away from that pattern. If I'm tempted to jump back in, I'll go to the lounge and write some more— or go take a walk if it's so bad that I have to get out of the building entirely.

▣ PLAN YOUR RESPONSE

What if the worst happens and people react negatively to your changes despite your careful preparation? Plan what your response will be to the worst-case scenario so you can approach change with confidence. When you've mentally anticipated and handled the worst that could happen, you no longer fear it.

Alice made these contingency plans for handling resistance that could come up in spite of her plans to minimize it:

Rick

If Rick gets angry, I won't fight back. I'll hear him out and ask if we can meet again when we've both had a chance to cool down and think things over. I'll be patient and wait out his anger until we can talk. Then I will have a much better chance of not reacting myself and of being heard by him. I will explain to him that I feel ineffective in directing Connie and Ed, since I am not in a supervisory role with them. I'll point out that the bottom line for me is that I don't feel good about the work that I am trained and hired to do when I think I'm being put in the position of supervising them.

If he goes silent on me, I'll tell him what I see happening. If he starts an underground campaign against me, I'll get Ellen in the Personnel Department to mediate.

Ed

If Ed gets angry, I will choose to stay calm and tell him that I want to talk about it when he is ready, as it is important I clarify what is happening. I'll stress to him that the current way I interact with him on the job doesn't work for me and that I'd like to change that. If that doesn't work, I'll get either Rick or Ellen to mediate.

Connie

If Connie shuts down and withdraws, I will tell her I feel shut out by her and unable to discuss problems. Failing my ability to engage her, I will maintain my stance—that her work is hers, and mine is mine—and do whatever I can to make our relationship more open and supportive. I won't push the issue, and I will ask her to coffee or stop by her desk to catch up with her occasionally.

Myself

If I catch myself reverting to old patterns, I may need to get away from the situation physically—to the lounge or for a walk—to write in my notebook and have a talk with myself. I'll ask myself if I really want to start that old pattern again, review the trouble it's caused me in the past, remember my resolve to stop, and envision how I want things to be from now on.

When you've taken these first five steps, you've prepared yourself as well as you can. Now it's time to make changes.

16

Step #6: Make the Change and Assess the Results

You've done all the preparation. Now it's time to make your first change—and take a quantum leap in the way you relate to people, to your work, and to success.

THE KEYS TO SUCCESS

As you start making changes, keep these tips in mind:

- *Keep breathing.* Change is threatening, and stress can actually cause shortness of breath, which creates even more stress. Breathing relaxes you and lets you think more clearly.

- *Timing is important.* You maximize your chances for success when you choose an appropriate time to discuss the problem or make the change.

* *Respect the other person.* Your attitude, tone of voice, and presence will be less threatening if you approach the other person with genuine respect.

* *Avoid all power plays.* Be careful not to use words or statements that might be interpreted as power-tripping, blaming, or humiliating. Use "I-Centered" Communication and avoid one-upmanship.

* *Give yourself permission* to break three rules that most of us learned in our families: Don't think about yourself, Always put others first, and Don't feel. As you make your changes, remember to think about yourself, put yourself first, and consider your feelings.

◙ JUMPING IN

You need to be prudent about making changes, but some people talk themselves into waiting forever. They are like swimmers shivering at the end of the diving board—afraid to jump in because the water is icy cold, but meanwhile freezing to death up on the board.

These people end up feeling like victims of their criticism, frustrated by their inability to make changes and waiting for improvements that never come. They feel paralyzed and powerless, unable to act or express themselves because they won't take the initiative and make unilateral changes.

If you wait for others to change with you, you may wait forever. It may not be fair that you have to go first and that no one else may follow, but it's the only way to take responsibility for your own success, self-esteem, satisfaction, and health—and to get what you want. The system won't move by itself; you have to move first.

◙ THE FOUR PHASES OF EVERY CHANGE

What actually happens when you start making changes? Understanding this process can help you proceed in the most effective way.

All emotional systems develop patterns—roles, rules, ways of relating—that provide a sense of equilibrium or homeostasis. Any change to these patterns can shake people up, inducing a sense of unpredictability and discomfort. *Everyone in the system feels some degree of stress when patterns change.* This is one of the major reasons why we are most likely to reach for what we know—old family patterns—during times of change.

Every change has four basic phases. No line marks where one phase ends and another begins; they flow together following this basic sequence:

1. Commitment: You decide to change. In Phase #1, you decide on a change and commit to it. You may feel anxious and uncomfortable because you are in uncharted territory. You may also feel resistance and be tempted to go back to your old ways. The people around you probably feel frustrated, defensive, and threatened because they sense you—and their relationship with you—will soon be moving out of their control.

2. Disorientation: You break the habit or pattern, and everybody loses his balance. This is the distressing time after you break the pattern, but before you replace it with a new behavior. You feel out of control and in constant motion. Your old balance with people is gone and no new balance has taken its place yet, so everybody feels like pieces of that mobile blowing in the wind. You all feel as if you are operating in the dark without the old reliable dynamics, unhealthy and unproductive as they may have been. This makes everyone feel confused, vulnerable, and wary, so old family emotional defenses are likely to surface.

Communication is very important at this point, but it is also very difficult. Phase #2 creates the most resistance because it is the most stressful and threatening. It takes courage to operate out of control, without handrails, until a new order is established.

3. Integration: The new behavior begins to emerge. The new behavior is still a little erratic and your new balance with others hasn't completely stabilized, but a new pattern is beginning to emerge. Everyone begins to see how things are going to be and starts adjusting to the new ways of relating. People may not have accepted your new behavior completely, and you may still experience some residual resistance and discontent, but the changes are starting to be integrated into your relationships.

Phase #3 is about holding the course until you have the results you want and appreciating and acknowledging those who have been willing to accept your changes.

4. Reorientation: Your new behaviors become habits. You don't have to think about the new behaviors anymore, and other people have become used to them as well. Your relationships have rebalanced and reoriented themselves to the changes you've made. Phase #4 is about enjoying what you've accomplished before you identify another behavior or relationship that you want to change—and a whole new cycle of change begins.

▣ ALICE'S CHANGES

Alice used the keys to successful changes and remembered the four phases of any change as she made these adjustments in her relationships at work:

Rick

On Monday morning, she met with Rick to present her new agenda. She began by saying that this job was important to her, so she'd worked out a few things that had been bothering her and wanted to share them with him and enlist his support.

She said she'd realized that one of the things that had made the promotional project so difficult was that she had drifted into being Ed and Connie's unofficial manager, and she thought that he could manage them much more effectively than she could. She said it was just too stressful for her to have that responsibility without the authority that went with it, and suggested that all four of them meet to stress that she, Connie, and Ed all worked for and were managed by Rick. She also asked that he not discuss their work with her unless it involved information she needed in order to do *her* work, but instead speak directly to them.

Alice told Rick that she knew she had a tendency to jump in and save everyone from disaster when there were problems, but that she knew that wasn't productive for any of them—and she asked for his help in breaking the habit.

Rick seemed quiet at first, so Alice asked what his reaction was to all of this. He hesitated, then asked, "Are you leaving?" Alice said that she had no intention of leaving, that in fact she wanted these changes so that she could stay. She explained that her intention was not to do less work, but to grow and to do more—and she realized she had to change in order to do that.

Rick was impressed and surprisingly supportive once she reassured him that she wasn't about to quit. He even tried to jump on the personal-growth bandwagon, saying that it would probably be good for him to manage Ed and Connie more directly. He agreed to all she asked and set a time for their four-way meeting to clarify the lines of authority and communication.

Alice left the meeting elated but somewhat stunned. Rick had actually seemed to understand her situation and to support her in making this change. She realized that perhaps she had uncovered another of her family patterns—expecting trouble from all directions even when there was no real reason to do so.

Ed

Alice set up separate meetings with Ed and Connie. She took Ed to coffee and apologized for being such a Tyrant during the promotional project. She admitted she had overstepped her authority with him and Connie and told him that she wanted a respectful, cooperative, and mutually supportive working relationship with him. Alice said she knew he might not trust her right away but invited him to watch her over the next few months and see that she meant what she said.

Ed got in a few gibes—"So you're still trying to run things, just in a nicer way?"—but Alice let them sail right past her and didn't fight back. She could tell he understood what she was saying and was actually fascinated by it, but that he didn't entirely believe her. She knew that she would have to prove through behavior that she meant business.

Connie

Alice took Connie out for lunch the same day and had essentially the same conversation with her. She apologized for her behavior, shared with Connie her tendency to charge in on a white horse, and said she wanted to break that habit. Alice said she'd talked with Rick about straightening out the lines of authority and asked him not to put her in that position again. She told Connie that what she wanted was a respectful, supportive relationship in which they operated independently but could work together in productive ways.

Connie nodded and even forced a smile at one point. Alice could tell that Connie had heard her but was suspicious. She said, "Connie, I know this seems like a big change, but I'm really committed to it. I know you may find that hard to believe, but watch my feet and give it a chance."

Connie agreed to do that and even smiled again.

Herself

Alice had to work hard to change her pattern. Strong feelings of frustration and anger arose when she saw Ed or Connie not getting their work done. In the past, she had masked or buried those feelings with power plays—usually bullying or intimidation—that put her back in control. Now she just had to sit with those feelings, remind herself that she wasn't responsible for Ed and Connie, or their work, and concentrate on her own tasks. She had judgments about them, but she reminded herself again that their level of competence was none of her business.

It was difficult at first, but also quite enlightening. Alice saw just how strong her patterns of judgment and tyranny were, but she also saw how destructive they had been—both to her colleagues and to herself. It was hard to keep from jumping back into those old patterns, just as it had been hard to break a habit she'd developed last year of stopping in for an apple fritter before work every day—but as with the apple fritter, she could see that giving it up would make her happier and healthier in the end.

◘ ALICE'S ASSESSMENTS

The second part of Step #6 is assessing your results.

The four-way meeting with Rick, Ed, Connie, and herself went extremely well, especially since Alice had laid the groundwork for it in her private meetings with Ed and Connie, and they all agreed to try the new regime. Rick began having regular meetings with Ed and Connie, and everyone started getting used to the new way of doing things.

Over the next few months, Alice experienced a few challenges. Twice, when minor emergencies arose, Rick called her in and asked how Ed and Connie were doing. Alice reminded him that he should ask *them,* and he smiled in agreement.

Connie and Ed were wary of Alice at first and kept their distance. She knew she had something to prove to them and fought daily battles within herself not to judge or pressure them. Sometimes she had to get away to the coffee shop with her notebook and write down everything she was thinking and feeling. She reminded herself that her patterns of bullying and rescuing had come from her family and were not effective reactions now. She wrote down a scenario of how she wanted to relate to Ed and Connie and listed the benefits of letting go of her patterns. Then she took a deep breath and went back to work.

After about a month, she found that she no longer had to do this. The new habits were taking hold, and she even found herself enjoying Ed and Connie's company. After about three months, everyone seemed to have found his or her place in the new pattern. They all felt more relaxed, the office ran more smoothly, and everybody felt like a bigger person.

Alice experienced a level of genuine self-esteem that she had never felt before. Despite being a Rescuer and Superachiever all her life, she had never felt fulfilled within herself or in control of her actions. Now she knew that she could take on an enormous internal challenge, and win.

◙ Alice's changes worked in part because she had prepared herself so well to make them and followed the Six Action Steps for Change. Not all changes work. You may encounter a system that is simply too rigid to change or an individual too entrenched in his or her ways to handle the changes you want to make in the relationship.

When this happens, step back and reassess what you are doing. Is there a better way to go about making the change? Is this a change you need to make now, or can it wait until later? Can you live with not making the change, or do you have to leave if it can't be made? Sometimes the change involves a close examination of the attitudes and beliefs you have about people. Alice later had to do this when she assessed her relationship with Earl and discovered that she held harsh judgments about older men, particularly military men. These are all questions that only you can answer, and they are part of the process of allowing yourself an emotional environment that supports your health, happiness, and success.

These Six Action Steps are designed to give you just that—relationships that are supportive, productive, and enjoyable. You may find other advantages as well, and some of them are described in the next chapter.

17

Hidden Perks

Congratulations! It takes courage and a deep commitment to yourself to examine your family patterns, let go of old habits, and make positive changes. Those shifts can be uncomfortable, even painful, but breaking the old mold gives you the freedom to create a new one that better supports the person you are now and what you want today.

One reward for your work will be richer, happier, healthier, and more productive work relationships, but there are some less obvious benefits as well.

◉ LEAVING YOUR FAMILY

You may have left home physically many years ago, but letting go of old family patterns is another kind of leaving home. It can be difficult because you're cutting old psychological bonds, however unhealthy, with people who may still be important to you. Sometimes releasing these unworkable, limiting behaviors can even feel like a betrayal of your family.

It's not, of course. It's just part of growing up and becoming your own person, with your own goals and visions. Just as you have to leave home in order to find your own life, you have to let go of your family's emotional patterns to find new, more effective ways of relating to others. The freedom you gain is psychological and emotional rather than merely physical. You begin to live life from a whole new perspective, one that reflects who you truly are, not the person whom you learned to be from them.

Releasing yourself from these old dynamics doesn't mean you don't love your family. It just means that those old patterns are no longer productive or appropriate for you—just as the clothes you wore as a child are no longer appropriate. It's time to get a whole new wardrobe, one that reflects the person you have become and lets you move forward in life.

▣ SELF-RESPONSIBILITY

Aldous Huxley said, "Experience is not what happens to you, but what you make of what happens to you." As you leave home behind and make choices that are less influenced by your family's patterns, you begin taking responsibility for your own experience of life. You are no longer a prisoner of the past or a victim of your family system. You become less concerned with defending yourself and fitting in and more concerned with discovering yourself and developing healthy relationships with others. You automatically become more centered and productive in the world.

Self-responsibility doesn't mean beating yourself up when things go wrong. It simply means understanding that you have the power to make choices and are accountable for yourself. It means becoming an adult who accepts difficulties as challenges to grow and bring forth new parts of yourself.

▣ BECOMING THE MAIN CHARACTER IN YOUR OWN LIFE

Knowing that you are your own person and capable of making choices and influencing events is the first step in becoming the main character in your own life. Many people never make this transition and live their entire lives as minor characters in other people's dramas. They remain forever focused on their parents, their children, their bosses, their coworkers, or their friends—not on themselves.

By focusing on your own life, I don't mean living a completely selfish existence with no concern for others. Being the main character in your own life simply means getting your own desires and wants fulfilled (which actually allows you to be more supportive of others), nurturing your relationships, and making sure that your life is exciting and productive.

▣ LETTING OTHERS LIVE THEIR OWN LIVES

The other side of this coin is allowing others to be the main characters in *their* own lives—letting them deal with their own challenges and follow their own lights.

This may mean letting them experience the discomfort they feel when you make changes in your relationship with them. My clients often feel guilty when their new behaviors hurt others or make them uncomfortable and are then tempted to return to their old behaviors. This is a crucial moment. Returning to old habits doesn't really take away other people's pain; it just eliminates the possibility for growth. By sticking to your changes, you let others pass through the challenge, grow, and come into a new and healthier relationship with you.

▣ FREEDOM

Not living your life for others or making them live their lives for you gives you a freedom unlike any other. You become calmer, more appreciative of yourself and others, and more open to new possibilities.

You are no longer at the mercy of your old family patterns or the way things are. You have the autonomy to create, to express, and to invent new ways of enjoying and relating to others. You can explore all the parts of yourself and choose how you want your relationships to be.

▣ PERSONAL POWER

When you know that you are in charge of your thoughts and emotions rather than at the mercy of old family patterns, you are in control of your own destiny. You understand that the problem is often not the situation itself but your reaction to it—and you know that you have dominion over those reactions. No matter what life puts in your path, you know you can handle it.

Knowledge is power, and the process of examining your family patterns gives you a strong dose of self-knowledge. You also have a strategy on which to model any change you want to make, in any area of your life.

Personal power means knowing that you have choices, and you now have choices you didn't have as a child. You understand how you are likely to react to certain situations, and also that you don't have to react in those ways. You can take time to assess your thoughts and feelings and decide on the best response.

Personal power is an inner strength that grows out of your courage to examine where you are and how you got there, and to make changes even when they are uncomfortable. This power extends beyond your ability to improve relationships at work. You can use it in all areas of your life.

▣ UNDERSTANDING RELATIONSHIPS

We have concentrated on work relationships in this book, but the same principles apply to all relationships. The exercises you have done here can also apply to friends, lovers, and family.

Whenever two or more people come together, an emotional environment develops. It can be mapped, understood, and changed just as you have done with work relationships in this book. The more you practice, the more skilled you become at creating relationships that are nurturing, loving, and supportive.

▣ SELF-AWARENESS AND SELF-EXPRESSION

The more you know about yourself, the more you can express—and the more open you become to knowing more.

As you become accustomed to speaking your own truths—to yourself and others—you no longer need to hide from tension, anxiety, or conflict. You can say what you feel and believe with confidence and with respect for the other person.

As children, most of us were not taught to value or express our own thoughts or feelings. In fact, it was better if we didn't even know our thoughts and feelings. We disrupted the family's emotional environment far less if we simply looked around us for what we should think and feel, rather than exploring what we actually did think and feel.

Those of us who grew up this way often have trouble finding our own thoughts and emotions, and even more trouble expressing them. We may even feel threatened and defensive in the presence of our own truths and find it difficult to be honest with ourselves and others. Discovering inner truths is part of the process of changing difficult work relationships. The ability to find and talk about these truths makes life richer, deepens our relationships with ourselves, and carries over into all other aspects of our lives.

▣ SELF-ESTEEM

Knowing who you are and being able to speak your truth to others is the essence of self-esteem. Most of us have to learn to trust and honor ourselves. It was not something we were taught at home.

Telling the truth about old, limiting family patterns and choosing to change them makes us trustworthy to ourselves. When we were at the mercy of these patterns, reacting defensively and automatically to any threat, we did not feel trustworthy or have self-respect.

Each time you choose not to react in unhealthy or stressful ways and redirect your energy into healing and enriching a relationship, you become more trustworthy to yourself and deepen your self-esteem. Each time you make a successful change, you reinforce that self-esteem.

◙ THE BENEFITS TO YOUR ORGANIZATION

You will be making these changes for yourself, not for your organization, but your organization will probably benefit as well—and whatever benefits your organization also benefits you .

Organizations become stronger and more flexible when they can stay open to the changes initiated by empowered employees, those who know they have choices and seek to resolve problems—those who have the courage to be honest.

Organizational leaders are seeing the benefits of openness and trust and encouraging self-awareness, self-expression, and self-respect among employees. In *Leadership Is an Art,* Max De Pree describes it as "fostering the intimacy of high-quality relationships." True leaders "walk the walk" of self-responsibility and openness themselves. Passion, commitment, and creativity flow naturally because people are motivated by the power of their own inner spirit.

In *The Fifth Discipline,* Peter E. Senge calls organizations that empower employees "learning organizations" that create a "conspiracy of authenticity" by supporting openness, humility, and willingness to change.

Will Schutz, a leader in organizational development and human relationships, characterizes the empowering organization in *The Truth Option* as one that creates an atmosphere of honesty, openness, and self-determination.

◙ THE GREATEST GIFT

It would be wonderful if your organization transformed overnight into one of these learning organizations, but that is not your job. Your only job is to discover yourself, express yourself, and fulfill your potential. That is the greatest gift you can give yourself or anyone else. Enjoy!

Bibliography

Allen, David M. *Unifying Individual and Family Therapies*. San Francisco: Jossey-Bass, 1987.

Becvar, Raphael J., and Dorothy Stroh Becvar. *Systems Theory and Family Therapy*. Lanham, MD: University Press of America, Inc., 1982.

Block, Peter. *The Empowered Manager*. San Francisco: Jossey-Bass, 1987.

Bolman, Lee G., and Terence E. Deal. *Modern Approaches to Understanding and Managing Organizations*. San Francisco: Jossey-Bass, 1984.

Borysenko, Joan. *Minding the Body, Mending the Mind*. New York: Bantam, 1988.

Constantine, Larry. *Family Paradigms*. New York: Guilford Press, 1986.

Kets de Vries, Manfred F. R., and Danny Miller. *The Neurotic Organization*. San Francisco: Jossey-Bass, 1984.

Kerr, Michael E., and Murray Bowen. *Family Evaluation*. New York: Norton, 1988.

Levering, Robert. *A Great Place to Work*. New York: Avon, 1988.

Friedman, Edwin H. *Generation to Generation.* New York: Guilford Press, 1985.

McGoldrick, M., and Randy Gerson. *Genograms in Family Assessment.* New York: Norton, 1985.

Mengel, M. B. "Physician Ineffectiveness Due to Family-of-Origin Issues." *Family Systems Medicine,* 5 (2), 176–190.

Palazzoli, Mara Selvini, et al. *The Hidden Games of Organizations.* New York: Pantheon Books, 1986.

Plas, Jeanne M., and Kathleen V. Hoover-Dempsey. *Working Up a Storm.* New York: Norton, 1988.

Rosenblatt, Paul C., Leni de Mik, Roxanne Marie Anderson, and Patricia A. Johnson. *The Family in Business.* San Francisco: Jossey-Bass, 1985.

Schaef, Anne Wilson, and Diane Fasel. *The Addictive Organization.* San Francisco: Harper & Row, 1988.

Schutz, Will. *The Truth Option.* Berkeley, CA: Ten Speed Press, 1984.

Senge, Peter M. *The Fifth Discipline.* New York: Doubleday/Currency, 1990.

Smith, Brian R., and Myrna M. Milani. *Beyond the Magic Circle: The Role of Intimacy in Business.* Unity, NH: Fainshaw Press, 1989.

Smith, Carol Cox. *Recovery at Work.* New York: Harper & Row, 1990.

Wegschieder, Sharon. *Another Chance.* Palo Alto: Science and Behavior Books, 1981.

Weinberg, Richard B., and Larry B. Mauksch. "Examining Family of Origin Influences in Life at Work." Paper delivered at the annual meeting of the American Association for Marriage and Family Therapy, San Francisco, October 1989.

Wynne, Lyman C., Susan H. McDaniel, and Timothy T. Webber, editors. *Systems Consultation: A New Perspective for Family Therapy.* New York: The Guilford Press, 1986.

Index